Vatican II
ITS IMPACT ON YOU

Peter A. Huff, PhD

Liguori
ONE LIGUORI DRIVE
LIGUORI MO 63057-9999

Imprimi Potest:
Harry Grile, CSsR, Provincial
Denver Province, The Redemptorists

Published by Liguori Publications
Liguori, Missouri 63057

To order, call 800-325-9521, or visit liguori.org

Library of Congress Cataloging-in-Publication Data

Huff, Peter A.
Vatican II : its impact on you / Peter A. Huff.—1st ed.
p. cm.
ISBN 978-0-7648-1915-5
1. Vatican Council (2nd : 1962-1965) I. Title. II. Title: Vatican 2.
BX8301962 .H785 2011
262'.52—dc23
2011031988

Liguori Publications, a nonprofit corporation, is an apostolate of the Redemptorists. To learn more about the Redemptorists, visit Redemptorists.com.

Printed in the United States of America
15 14 13 12 11 / 5 4 3 2 1
First Edition

Contents

Preface

This book is for people who want a brief overview of Vatican II and its impact on our lives today. It is primarily designed for adult lay Catholics and newcomers to the Church, converts, and catechumens in RCIA programs. Christians in other communions who want to know more about the Second Vatican Council and seekers who want to be better acquainted with the contemporary Catholic experience will also profit from this book.

The book is written from a Catholic perspective. At the same time, I take very seriously what the council teaches about the need to work for Christian unity. I also take seriously what it says about "elements of truth and grace" in all the religions of the world. I hope readers will find in the book an ecumenical spirit and an invitation to dialogue.

Many people have helped me understand Vatican II. I especially want to thank Professor Ronald Modras, who first introduced me to the council's theology in a doctoral seminar at Saint Louis University, and the professors who taught him the meaning of the council: Hans Kung and Joseph Ratzinger (Pope Benedict XVI).

Scriptural quotations come from the *New Revised Standard Version* of the Bible. Vatican II quotations are taken from the edition of the council documents prepared by the late Father Austin Flannery; each citation includes the abbreviation of the document's Latin title and the relevant numbered section of the text. Unless otherwise noted, the other Church documents cited in the book—papal encyclicals and other texts—can be found on the Vatican Web site at vatican.va.

ABBREVIATIONS OF VATICAN II DOCUMENTS

(AA)   *Apostolicam Actuositatem:* Decree on the Apostolate of the Laity

(AG)   *Ad Gentes:* Decree on the Church's Missionary Activity

(CD)   *Christus Dominus:* Decree on the Bishops' Pastoral Office in the Church

(DH)   *Dignitatis Humanae:* Declaration on Religious Freedom

(DV)   *Dei Verbum:* Dogmatic Constitution on Divine Revelation

(GE)   *Gravissimum Educationis:* Declaration on Christian Education

(GS)   *Gaudium et Spes:* Pastoral Constitution on the Church in the Modern World

(IM)   *Inter Mirifica:* Decree on the Instruments of Social Communication

(LG)   *Lumen Gentium:* Dogmatic Constitution on the Church

(NA)   *Nostra Aetate:* Declaration on the Relationship of the Church to Non-Christian Religions

(OE)   *Orientalium Ecclesiarum:* Decree on Eastern Catholic Churches

(OT)   *Optatam Totius:* Decree on Priestly Formation

(PC)   *Perfectae Caritatis:* Decree on the Appropriate Renewal of the Religious Life

(PO)   *Presbyterorum Ordinis:* Decree on the Ministry and Life of Priests

(SC)   *Sacrosanctum Concilium:* Constitution on the Sacred Liturgy

(UR)   *Unitatis Redintegratio:* Decree on Ecumenism

Introduction

Ask any number of Catholics anywhere on the planet and you are bound to get the same response. What event, more than any other, has had the greatest impact on the Catholic experience today? The answer: Vatican II.

Probe for detail, interpretation, or commentary, and you are just as likely to see what promised to be an engaging conversation come to an abrupt and awkward conclusion. Catholics know the Second Vatican Council ranks high on the scale of religious and cultural importance. It is a crucial part of our spiritual identity, we say. But all too often we are short on context and skimpy on specifics.

Some Catholics may be able to tell you what it was like to live through the dramatic years of the council. Younger Catholics may single it out as the prime reason their experience seems so different from that of their grandparents. Converts may even get the impression that the Church they are entering is not the same as the one portrayed in history books and old movies—and all because of something called Vatican II.

But what exactly was Vatican II? Why was it so important? And why does it still exert such tremendous influence on Catholic life?

This book will introduce you to the remarkable events and personalities of the Second Vatican Council and the inspiring documents that those events and personalities produced. It will also introduce you to the thrust of Catholic history—almost twenty centuries of it—that made the events, personalities, and documents of the council possible. Most importantly, it will invite you to reflect on the meaning of Vatican II for your life today and for the future of our Church.

The book tells the story of Vatican II. It analyzes its sources, its context, its decisions, and its ongoing impact. It does not, however, perpetuate myths about the council or belabor the difference between its so-called "spirit" and the "letter" of its documents. Vatican II was neither the high point of Christian history nor the self-destruction of Catholic tradition. We rightly associate the council with change, but it is just as correctly portrayed as a strategic preservation of Catholicism's time-tested heritage.

Vatican II was one council among others. Major Church councils preceded it. Others could follow. As Catholics we always need to take the long view of history. Over time, Vatican II will find its rightful place in the adventure of faith we call salvation history.

No one can deny, though, that Vatican II has made us the sort of Catholics we are now. It is one in a long line of councils, but it is most assuredly *our* council, the council for our times. That is why we cannot stop thinking about it, talking about it, even arguing about it.

In the middle of the twentieth century, after World War II gave way to history's first superpower standoff, the 261st successor of the Apostle Peter summoned his brother bishops from around the world to a solemn assembly of prayer, worship, and pastoral decision-making. Led by the Holy Spirit and under the special protection of Saint Joseph, patron of the council, they read the "signs of the times" and reexamined Catholic Christianity's mission in light of what they called "the joy and hope, the grief and anguish of the men of our time" (*GS* 1). It was the most important religious event of the twentieth century.

This assembly of some 2,500 bishops met in Vatican City's magnificent Basilica of Saint Peter's during four sessions over the course of three years, from the fall of 1962 to Advent in 1965. The bishops were assisted by an elite corps of theologians and energized by the presence of all sorts of special guests and scores of reporters, not to mention untold numbers of pilgrims and well-wishers from all over the earth.

Blessed John XXIII, the pope who convened the council, urged his fellow bishops to make the meeting a "wonderful spectacle of truth, unity, and charity" (*Ad Petri Cathedram*, 62). It was that and much more. Participants and eyewitnesses spoke of it as a new Pentecost, a modern-day reenactment of that spring morning two millennia earlier when the Holy Spirit first descended upon the Church of Jesus Christ.

It was the spiritual experience of a lifetime. It was also a major media event. Vatican II was the first Catholic council in history to be covered by radio and television.

Photographs and films of the event transport us back to an age of snowy black-and-white TV sets and computers as big as classrooms, a world with no fast food and no cell phones. For some people, Vatican II represents nothing more than a Catholic "Camelot," forever lost. Others dismiss it as near-ancient history. Seen through the eyes of faith, though, those pictures teach us a great deal about the mysterious way in which the eternal God leads his Church through every phase of its earthly pilgrimage. He is still leading us today.

If there is one lesson Vatican II keeps driving home, it is this: Ours is a living faith and a living Church. Pope John called the Church "forever young" (*Ad Petri Cathedram*, 2).

The impact of Vatican II has been enormous. We feel its influence in every dimension of our faith experience—from our patterns of worship and religious education to our assumptions about authority, freedom, and moral responsibility. We see its effects all around us, in the dioceses, parishes, schools, hospitals, charities, media outlets, and other organizations that make up the Catholic institutional land-scape. We perceive the full extent of its impact when we reflect on our relationship to the world beyond the walls of the Church. Vatican II transformed the way we think about science, politics, economics, art, non-Christian religions, and the varieties of unbelief in contemporary society—the entire range of interests proper to human beings created in the image of God.

The council's influence is especially evident in our basic under-standing of what it means to be Catholic. No part of present-day Catholicism makes sense without reference to the vision and legacy of the Second Vatican Council. Even the current vocations crisis and the clergy sex abuse scandal become comprehensible only when set in the context of the era inaugurated by Vatican II.

Millions of Catholics around the globe are right. No event has had a greater impact on Catholic experience today than Vatican II. The world of those council fathers—the modern Church's "greatest generation"—is still very much our world. Their concerns are still our concerns. Computers are smaller now, and phones are about as mobile as they can get. Their Cold War is a closed chapter of history, almost as exotic as the War of the Roses or China's Boxer Rebellion. But the human community's sense of "grief and anguish" is just as palpable, just as heart-rending—maybe even more so. Violence, injustice, and the struggle to find meaning in life continue to define our experience in the twenty-first century.

The event called Vatican II, known to every Catholic at least by name, shows us who we are, what we stand for, and what we need to live for. A fresh encounter with its idealism and its insight will reacquaint us with the source of our joy and hope. It is still the council for our times.

CHAPTER ONE
The Impact of Councils

Vatican II was not the first council in Catholic history, and it will probably not be the last. Councils have played a vital role in the Catholic story since the beginning. In fact, it is hard to imagine Catholicism without councils. Without them we would not have the Nicene Creed, a sevenfold sacramental system, or a method for calculating the date for Easter. We would not have a formal doctrine of transubstantiation or papal infallibility. We might not even have a Catholic Bible.

Councils represent a distinctively Catholic approach to Christian experience. A *conciliar*, or council-related, principle lies at the heart of what it means to be Catholic. Everybody knows that the Catholic Church is not a democracy. Still, a form of collective decision-making is built into the Catholic way of doing things. Councils teach us that Christianity is a group project. It is not a faith for lone individuals, nor is it a dictatorship. We live our faith in the context of a vast network of believers, a universal family stretching across the globe and even back through time and up into heaven. We pray, as the liturgy says, with "all the Angels and Saints, and you, my brothers and sisters." Councils are one way the Catholic community takes care of its earthly business.

At its most basic, a council is an official gathering of Church leaders seeking, with the help of the Holy Spirit, to solve a problem, answer a question, or renew the Church's mission in light of changing or threatening circumstances not anticipated by the New Testament writers. The term general or *ecumenical* council (from the Greek for "whole world") refers to an extraordinary meeting of all the Church's bishops assembled for the purpose of exercising their God-given authority as they address a new issue or challenge. Twenty-one such councils, each named after the location of its meeting, have punctuated the long and eventful history of the Catholic Church.

The first ecumenical council was held in AD 325 at Nicea (now a city in modern-day Turkey). It gave us the Nicene Creed, the most significant document in Christian literature next to the Bible. Vatican II, held more than 1,600 years later, was the most recent council in the series. Eastern Orthodox Churches and some Protestant denominations recognize as authoritative the first seven councils. Many evangelical Christians with their "Bible only" doctrine reject the entire notion of Church councils. For Catholics, all twenty-one ecumenical councils represent major milestones in the formation of Catholic doctrine and practice.

Jesus Promises the Advocate

The Catholic concept of councils is based on two important convictions: (1) Christianity was not a finished product in the first century, and (2) our Lord did not abandon his Church after the ascension. Blessed John Henry Newman, the famous convert-cardinal of the 1800s, captured the first of these convictions in his idea of the development of doctrine. The Church, he said, is like the Virgin Mary, who "treasured all these things in her heart" (Luke 2:51). The apostles proclaimed the Gospel in its essentials. Over the centuries, the Church's understanding of the Gospel treasure matured. Catholic teachings such as purgatory and the Immaculate Conception, not explicitly mentioned in the Bible, were present in seed form in early Christian preaching and devotion. Catholics believe that this process of development still goes on today. We do not look simply to the letter of Scripture but to the living tradition of the Church, the body of Christ.

Saint Paul spoke quite favorably of tradition (see 1 Corinthians 11:2 and 2 Thessalonians 2:15). Tradition (from the Latin for "handing on" the faith) should never be confused with man-made ideas and customs. Doctrinal development is not the product of mere human intellect or ingenuity. Nor is it adaptation to cultural trends. Human reason and intuition are involved in the process, but so is God's care for his Church. Ultimately the Church's deepening insights into the "mystery of the faith" (1 Timothy 3:9) are governed by God himself. Jesus promised his apostles that the Father would send the Advocate, or Holy Spirit, to "teach you everything" (John 14:26). "When the Spirit of truth comes," he said, "he will guide you into all the truth" (John 16:13). The Christian life is the ongoing exploration of God's infinite truth.

Jesus also empowered his apostles to teach the truth with authority and make judgments on disputed questions. He gave Saint Peter the "keys of the kingdom" with the right to "bind" and "loose" on earth and in heaven (Matthew 16:19). He bestowed similar powers upon all the apostles (Matthew 18:18), including the ability to forgive and retain sins (John 20:23). As successors of the apostles, popes and bishops share these same gifts and embody for their own age the sacred authority present at the birth of the Church.

The idea of councils is based on a high view of the Church. Though composed of ordinary human beings, too often weak and imperfect, the Church is a divinely ordained institution authorized to speak and enact the truth of God. Each generation of believers leaves its mark on the Church's understanding of the faith and the Christian vocation in the world. The dynamic force shaping the ever-expanding mind of the Church is always the Holy Spirit.

Councils in the Apostolic Age

We speak of the Council of Nicea as the first ecumenical council, and rightly so. It was a critical turning point in the evolution of Christianity, but it was not unprecedented. Catholicism's conciliar principle actually appears much earlier in the Christian story. In the Acts of the Apostles, we find two examples of how Church leaders gathered in council-like fashion to seek the will of the Holy Spirit and apply their authority to a serious issue facing the Christian community. These events set the stage for all future councils.

The first issue was the suicide of Judas Iscariot. Addressing a large group of disciples, including Mary and other women, Peter encouraged the fledgling Church to fill the betrayer's place in the brotherhood of the apostles with another suitable individual (Acts 1:21–22). The assembly agreed on two candidates, prayed for God's leadership, and then cast lots, confident that God would show them the right course of action. As Saint Luke tells us, "the lot fell on Matthias; and he was added to the eleven apostles" (Acts 1:26). This method would be repeated many times throughout the history of the Church: collective discernment coupled with prayer to a God who intervenes in human experience. In this case, it resolved Christianity's first crisis.

The same combination of group decision-making and divine guidance is a feature of the apostolic summit called the Council at Jerusalem. Around AD 50, the Church confronted an unexpected challenge: the conversion of gentiles (non-Jews) to faith in Christ. Should these new believers keep the Jewish law? Or could someone be a Christian without also being Jewish? The early Christians, all originally Jewish, were divided. At stake was the question of Christian identity. Is a Christian a Jew who accepts the Messiah? Or do Christians represent a "new humanity" (Ephesians 2:15)?

Luke describes the meeting of the apostles and elders called to tackle the problem—a meeting that involved "much debate" (Acts 15:7). Peter again took the lead, already convinced through contact with gentiles that "God shows no partiality" (Acts 10:34). Paul also spoke up for the newcomers, testifying to "signs and wonders" among the pagans (Acts 15:12). Leaders in the Hebrew-Christian community in Jerusalem defended the importance of Old Testament law in Christian life.

Saint James, the first bishop of Jerusalem, brought the meeting to its historic conclusion. From this point on, gentile converts would enjoy full Church membership with no obligation to observe the complete range of Jewish legislation. By the end of its first hundred years, Christianity was a gentile movement rapidly spreading into parts of the world where Judaism had never penetrated. The council at Jerusalem was a watershed moment in world history.

What especially strikes us here is a phrase used by the apostles in their letter to their new gentile brothers and sisters: "For it has seemed good to the Holy Spirit and to us..." (Acts 15:28). A simple yet remarkably bold formula, it expressed the apostles' desire to align the will of the young Church with the sometimes unpredictable and often mysterious will of God. Driven by this same holy ambition, future councils would change history, too.

From Nicea to Chalcedon

The Book of Acts ends with Saint Paul awaiting trial in pagan Rome (see Acts 28:16–31). The anti-Christian empire—"Babylon" in the New Testament (Revelation 17:5)—put the brakes on Church councils for nearly three centuries. Roman authorities made a point of targeting Church leaders. The plan was to decapitate the movement "turning the world upside down" (Acts 17:6). Popes and bishops swelled the ranks of martyrs.

An event in the early 300s changed everything. Constantine's conversion to Christianity dramatically transformed the Church's position in society and its prospects for the future. As emperor, he called off the persecution and started the process that would make Christianity the official religion of the empire. For the first time, Christians could contemplate what a Christian civilization might look like.

We should see the early ecumenical councils as products of a culture-building Church. The bishops who participated in the meetings were not leaders of a fringe cult. They were courageous and creative thinkers translating into terms meaningful to the best minds of their day the faith "once for all entrusted to the saints" (Jude 3). They were also practical administrators setting policy for a Church eager to carry out its mission in the world.

The importance of the Council of Nicea cannot be overstated. Convened by Constantine himself, the council was charged with settling a question at the core of the Christian world view: the true identity of Jesus Christ. The Church had already contended with Docetism (based on the Greek for "appearance"), a heresy that denied Christ's humanity. Now, his divinity was under assault. Named after Arius, the Egyptian priest who popularized it, the new Arian heresy demoted the Son of God to the status of a creature inferior to God the Father.

The bishops at Nicea knew that the faith was on the line. Intense deliberation lasted weeks. Arius made his case and secured some support. Another North African, a young deacon known to history as Saint Athanasius, rallied the opposition. Scripture and the consistent teaching of the Church, he argued, contradict the half-god of Arius. Logic does, too. A partially divine Savior cannot redeem a fully sinful humanity.

In the end, the council condemned Arianism and affirmed Christ as "one in Being" or "consubstantial" with the Father. With this insight as its cornerstone, the Nicene Creed grew into the great monument to truth that we cherish today. The next three general councils—Constantinople (381), Ephesus (431), and Chalcedon (451)—only strengthened the Church's witness to the cardinal mysteries of the faith: the Holy Trinity (one God in three persons) and the Incarnation (God made man). Other councils have rivaled Nicea in drama and passion. None has had a greater impact on what we believe.

Councils of the Middle Ages

The principle of councils was firmly established in the Catholic mind by the 400s. So was the institution of the papacy. Saint Leo the Great, the pope who dissuaded Attila the Hun from attacking Rome, played a decisive role in achieving consensus at the Council of Chalcedon. His letter to the assembly on the humanity and divinity of Jesus sparked enthusiastic cries of support from the council floor, inspiring the fathers to see the authority of Peter in the decisions of Leo. Since that time, the attempt to coordinate the authority of the Bishop of Rome with the authority of the world's bishops in council has been a hallmark of Catholic organizational life and *canon law* (Church law).

After Chalcedon, ecumenical councils, often called by the pope, met at a variety of locations and for a variety of reasons. Issues requiring attention included friction between popes and secular leaders, the *schism* (division) between the Eastern Churches and the Roman Church, schisms within the Western Church itself, the claims of false popes, and crusades to restore Christian custody of the Holy Land. Councils also reviewed problems of Church discipline, from the supervision of priests to the treatment of heretics.

The Fourth Lateran Council (1215) stands out as one of the most important Church meetings of the Middle Ages. Innocent III, the pope who approved the new Franciscan and Dominican orders, presided over the gathering, one of the largest in Catholic history. Held at the pope's cathedral church in Rome, the council focused mainly on sacramental topics. The bishops discussed the problems of mixed marriages (between Christians and Jews or Muslims) and the obligation of every Catholic to receive holy Communion at least once a year.

The bishops also contributed to the development of the theology of the Eucharist. Belief in the Real Presence of Christ in the Eucharist dates from earliest Christian times. Saint Paul spoke of a mystical "sharing" in the Body and Blood of Christ (1 Corinthians 10:16). Around AD 100, the bishop-martyr Saint Ignatius of Antioch called the Eucharist the "medicine of immortality" (*CCC* 1405). Lateran IV employed a new term to describe the process by which bread and wine are transformed into the literal presence of Christ on the altar: transubstantiation. Saint Thomas Aquinas translated this technical point of doctrine into the poetry of his hymn "*Adoro Te Devote*":

> *Godhead here in hiding, whom I do adore*
> *Masked by these bare shadows, shape and nothing more,*
> *See, Lord, at thy service low lies here a heart*
> *Lost, all lost in wonder at the God thou art* (CCC 1381).

From Trent to Vatican I

During the Middle Ages, ecumenical councils met on average about every fifty years. They have occurred with less frequency in the last 500 years. Council assemblies have tended to be larger, though, and have been greatly affected by advances in international transportation and mass communication. The two councils preceding Vatican II—Trent (1545–63) and Vatican I (1869–70)—set the pace for Catholic life and thought in the modern world.

The Council of Trent, held in the Italian town of Tridentum, or Trento, responded to the crisis of the Protestant Reformation. Martin Luther's criticism of lax morality in the Church, expressed in his *95*

Theses of 1517, quickly escalated into revolt against Catholic tradition. Protestantism gave birth to a streamlined Christianity focusing on the Bible and the individual. Social unrest spread along with the movement. The distinctively Catholic approach to Christianity, rooted in culture, sacrament, and ancient wisdom, was at risk.

The bishops at Trent answered Protestant charges with a defense of Christian tradition. Dodging fire, sword, and epidemic, the council fathers carried out their business during three periods: 1545–47, 1551–52, and 1562–63. Their decrees reaffirmed doctrines challenged by the reformers: original sin, justification, the seven sacraments, saints and images, and the traditional *canon* (list) of inspired scriptural books (including the Apocrypha or Deuterocanonical books eliminated from Protestant Bibles). The council also set an agenda for reform in the Catholic spirit, stressing priestly education, missionary activism, and artistic creativity. Often referred to as Counter-Reformation or Tridentine, this era of Church history generated an impressive roster of saints that includes some of our most cherished models of holiness: Teresa of Avila, John of the Cross, Ignatius Loyola, Francis Xavier, Francis de Sales, Vincent de Paul, and many others.

Nearly 300 years later, the First Vatican Council met during another period of radical change. By the 1800s, even Protestantism was on the defensive. Revolution was redrawing the map of Europe, and skepticism was eroding time-honored convictions. The council itself was interrupted by a clash of arms. Surrounded by the troops of a newly unified Italy, Pope Pius IX became the "prisoner of the Vatican."

Vatican I responded to the modern crisis of religious authority in two ways. First, it underscored the power of reason to reach beyond the limits of nature. God, the bishops declared, can be known from the evidence of the created world by the "natural light of human reason" (*CCC* 36). Second, the council reasserted the divine origin of the Church's *magisterium* (teaching office), especially as exercised by the pope. Belief in the primacy of Rome stems from the recognition of Saint Peter as the "rock" upon which Christ built his Church (Matthew 16:18) and the shepherd appointed to feed the Good Shepherd's sheep (John 21:15–17). Vatican I formally defined the infallibility of the

Roman pontiff as the gift of God protecting the pope from error when he proclaims essential matters of faith and morals *ex cathedra* ("from the chair" of the chief apostle)—that is, when he solemnly addresses core doctrines in his unique role as universal pastor. In an age of uncertainty, the First Vatican Council reconfirmed Catholic confidence in Christ's pledge to guide his Church "into all the truth" (John 16:13) and the sure leadership of the Holy Spirit to make that promise a reality.

CHAPTER TWO
The Prelude to Vatican II

Few people expected another council after Vatican I (known for many years as simply *the* Vatican Council). It seemed to be the Church's ultimate ecumenical council, theologically the most decisive and chronologically the end of the line. After the proclamation of papal infallibility, why would another council ever be necessary?

A major council in the twentieth century, and a second at the Vatican, came as a surprise to many people. Even bishops were caught off-guard. Vatican II, however, did not come out of nowhere. Movements of renewal and controversy within the Church paved the way for a new and different sort of council. So did nearly a century of unequaled social change. By the 1950s, it was clear that "*the* Vatican Council" was not the last word on the Church in the modern world.

The Catholic Literary Revival

The Catholic Literary Revival of the early twentieth century established a pattern of spirited Catholic engagement with all things modern. This flowering of Catholic cultural life gave us an extraordinary group of intellectuals, artists, and social critics whose works are now recognized as classics of unrivaled brilliance. G.K. Chesterton, Francois Mauriac, Evelyn Waugh, and many other writers laced their modern poetry and fiction with countercultural themes from the treasury of Catholic thought. As modern-day *apologists* ("defenders" of the faith), they offered a generation raised on doubt compelling reasons to believe. Motivated by the new social *encyclicals* (papal letters) of Popes Leo XIII and Pius XI, they also issued a call for justice in an industrial society increasingly characterized by materialism and greed.

The Catholic Revival was especially notable for its promotion of lay involvement in world affairs. Laypeople like the publishing couple Frank Sheed and Maisie Ward were the movement's heart and soul. Newman's spiritual autobiography *Apologia Pro Vita Sua* (1864) inspired a steady stream of pilgrims seeking the fullness of Christianity in Rome. Some of the West's brightest and best, disillusioned with the promises of the secular city, embraced the faith despite high levels of anti-Catholic prejudice in popular culture. For converts such as social activist Dorothy Day and priest-apologist Ronald Knox, the Church was the sole champion of sanity in a world veering dangerously toward madness.

The Modernist Crisis

The giants of the Catholic Literary Revival had mixed feelings about the modern world. Developments in education, social reform, transportation, and communication seemed to foster the very values that made Catholicism "catholic," or universal. The growing secularism of modern culture, on the other hand, raised the disturbing prospect of an entire civilization going about its business without God. The brutality of World War I forced many Catholics to come to grips with the dark side of modern experience.

The debate over modern ideas was particularly vigorous in the seminaries. Liberal Protestants had introduced "higher criticism" into theological education during the 1800s. This new approach viewed the Bible as the relic of an outdated world view, not a record of divine revelation. By the turn of the century, some Catholic theologians were also advocating more scientific methods in the study of Scripture and Church history. Called modernists, they wanted to reconcile Catholicism with the spirit of the age. A handful of modernists gave the impression of denying the authority of the Bible, the uniqueness of Christianity, and the divinity of Christ.

Pope Pius X condemned modernism in 1907. He accused the modernists of discounting reason, overemphasizing religious experience, and blindly accepting new scientific theories. As a result, priestly training entered a period of crisis, and a climate of suspicion spread throughout the seminaries. The curriculum was reduced to unchallenging handbooks. Few professors pursued original research. All clergy were required to take an anti-modernist oath.

To critics inside and outside the Church, Vatican reaction to modernism looked like the closing of the Catholic mind. Religious orders, though, still produced one exceptional scholar after another. Passionate lay writers continued to defend Catholic principles in the marketplace of ideas. Many took encouragement from their Church's crackdown on modernism. Catholicism was a much-needed alternative to the confusion and cynicism of modern life. Even with the conflict over modernism, the period between the Vatican councils was a phase of Catholic intellectual history marked by boundless energy and rare genius.

The Renewal of Liturgy

One sign of continuing vitality in Catholic culture was a new liturgical movement. The eucharistic miracle happens every day on altars around the globe, and Catholic worship ever points to the splendor of the unchanging truth of the Word made flesh (John 1:14). The Church's liturgy, however, has never been a static set of rites and readings. The Mass has developed over the course of Christianity's history.

The modern liturgical movement began in the 1800s. The Mass endorsed by the Council of Trent—the Tridentine Mass—was by then a thing of legend, a marvel of Catholic imagination and culture. The complexity of its order and the effectiveness of its celebration, however, were never above critique or modification. Many Catholic scholars wanted to recapture the spirit of prayer and praise that had so richly informed the lives of martyrs and saints in centuries before the Counter-Reformation. Their goal was to reclaim the original dignity and simplicity of what Saint Paul called our "spiritual" or "reasonable" worship (Romans 12:1).

Driving these efforts was the pastoral realization that sacramental worship is one of the most potent forces contributing to Catholic spiritual health and self-understanding. Leaders in the liturgical movement recognized the wisdom of the ancient saying, *Lex orandi, lex credendi*: "The law of prayer is the law of faith" (*CCC* 1124). How we worship makes us who we are.

Scholars in religious orders were especially interested in cultivating fresh appreciation for the Church's liturgical heritage. Benedictines made a singular impact on the movement. Monastic pioneers in Europe sparked a revival of Gregorian chant, advocated lay participation in the Mass, and raised liturgical literacy among ordinary believers. In the United States, Father Virgil Michel emphasized the moral link between the body of Christ in worship and Catholic social action in the world.

Laypeople responded energetically to the call for renewal. They upgraded church art, architecture, and music at the local level and organized international eucharistic congresses. A flood of print resources—missals, hymnals, and prayer books in Latin and the vernacular—inaugurated a new era of liturgical education and began to revolutionize the position of the layperson in the Church.

Rome blessed the movement, too. Pius X established schools to promote sacred song. His enthusiasm for daily Communion and his decree lowering first Communion age from adolescence to childhood profoundly affected Catholic life. Pius XII compared the liturgical movement to a sacred wind blowing through the Church. His encyclicals *Mystici Corporis Christi* (on the Church) and *Mediator Dei* (on liturgy) highlighted the supernatural quality of worship and the need to safeguard its holiness in an age increasingly tone-deaf to the sacred. He revised the Holy Week liturgy, reinstituted the Easter Vigil, relaxed the eucharistic fast (from several hours to three), and approved experiments with congregational singing, modern music, vernacular languages, evening Masses, and "dialogue" Masses (with laypeople reciting the responses). Today we see the achievements of Pius XII as important preparations for Vatican II's best-known liturgical reforms.

The Rediscovery of the Bible

The quest to retrieve the nobility and beauty of the liturgy included a rediscovery of the crucial place of the Bible in the Mass and the overall significance of worship in the Bible. All of this coincided with an explosion of interest in the Bible itself, intensified by sensational discoveries such as the Dead Sea Scrolls in the 1940s. The world wanted answers to questions about the Bible's origins, its meaning, and its authority in the age of science. Catholic interest in Scripture shot up to its highest point since the Reformation.

Vatican I reasserted belief in the Bible's uniqueness and its divine authorship. It also reconfirmed Saint Jerome's Latin translation, the Vulgate, as the official Bible for Catholic worship. After the council, the Church clarified standards for a method of interpretation that would properly honor divine revelation and meet the needs of the times. "Higher criticism" and modernism, based on private judgment and denial of the supernatural, were ruled out from the start. The challenge was to develop an approach to Scripture faithful to Church tradition and the best of modern historical methods at the same time.

Again, the papacy provided decisive leadership. Leo XIII published the first encyclical on modern biblical interpretation in 1893. His conviction that scientific truth can never really contradict scriptural truth greatly boosted Catholic confidence in the potential of dialogue with the modern mind. Fifty years later, Pius XII's encyclical *Divino Afflante Spiritu* commissioned scholars to produce vernacular translations and encouraged laypeople to make Bible reading a more fundamental part of their spiritual practice. Both popes wanted to strengthen biblical studies in seminary education. Both adopted Jerome's motto, "Ignorance of the Scriptures is ignorance of Christ" (*CCC* 133)—a theme destined to be a keynote of the Vatican II experience.

New organizations in the Church put flesh and bones on the Holy Fathers' intentions. Leo's Pontifical Biblical Commission and the Jesuit-run Pontifical Biblical Institute, both based in Rome, became world-renowned centers for scholarship in archaeology and ancient languages. Franciscan and Dominican authorities created similar institutions in the land of the Bible itself.

New translations delivered the fruit of these efforts to readers around the world. The Douay-Rheims version had well-served English-speaking Catholics since the 1500s. The Confraternity of Christian Doctrine (CCD), Pius X's initiative in *catechesis* (religious education), released a popular revision of the Douay-Rheims Bible in the 1940s. Monsignor Ronald Knox's one-man translation of the Vulgate also achieved critical acclaim among experts and a rising class of educated laypeople. Encounters with the Bible were reshaping the experience of twentieth-century Catholics in unexpected ways. A new generation of theologians was especially eager to reconnect the Church with its roots in the "living and active" word of God (Hebrews 4:12).

The "New Theology"

Scholars promoting rediscovery of the Bible were part of a movement called the "new theology" (*la nouvelle theologie*). They reinvigorated Catholic spirituality through a recovery of the style and world view of Christianity's first theologians: the biblical writers and Church Fathers. Their watchword was *ressourcement* (return to the sources). Catholics could find their way in the secular age, they said, only by going back to the forms of life and thought that gave the Christian tradition its original vitality and appeal.

Between the Vatican councils, the "new theologians" occupied a minority position in Catholic culture. The dominant school of thought was Thomism, named after Saint Thomas Aquinas. Since the late 1800s, nearly every worker in the intellectual apostolate, from professor to poet, had accepted Thomism as the basic frame of reference for the Catholic mind. Leo XIII elevated Thomism to the Church's favored philosophy. Subsequent popes declared it a reliable guide to scientific questions and an effective defense against error. Pius XII's *Humani Generis* (1950) endorsed a "return to the sources" but reaffirmed the method of Aquinas as Catholicism's "perennial" or permanent philosophy. Priest-scholar Reginald Garrigou-Lagrange, doctoral advisor of the future John Paul II, personified modern Thomism at its peak. Eminent laymen Jacques Maritain and Etienne Gilson produced versions of the philosophy that even secular critics found captivating.

Thomism erected impressive systems of abstract rationality based on mathematically precise distinctions between nature and grace. The "new theology" explored another side of religion: the intersection of nature and grace in concrete life situations. Drawing from the more poetic outlook of Scripture and patristic literature, the movement sought to understand the drama of faith in the dynamic contexts of historical change and human experience.

Four Frenchmen, two Dominicans, and two Jesuits gave the *nouvelle theologie* its distinctive character. Marie-Dominique Chenu shed new light on Saint Thomas himself, redefining Thomism as a thirteenth-century summary of faith, not a timeless set of truths. Yves Congar enriched Catholic *ecclesiology* (the doctrine of the Church), reexamining neglected topics such as Church unity and reform. Henri de Lubac and Jean Danielou stimulated new interest in Christian mysticism with their research on the Greek Fathers Origen and Gregory of Nyssa.

What made the "new theologians" so provocative was their appreciation for diversity in the Christian tradition. No matter how extraordinary, they said, Aquinas represented only one voice in the vast and venerable chorus of Catholic hearts and minds.

The scholars of the *nouvelle theologie* drew criticism from Church authorities. Careers were interrupted and orthodoxy questioned. After the election of Pope John XXIII, a Church historian in his own right, their ideas gained greater acceptance. Three leaders were invited to participate in the commissions that planned Vatican II. Two served as theological advisors at the council. Three were eventually named cardinals.

The story of the *nouvelle theologie* reminds us just how lively Catholic intellectual culture was between the Vatican councils. The "return to the sources" played a decisive role in setting the tone for the Second Vatican Council and its documents. Without the "new theology," Vatican II would have been a very different sort of council.

The Quest for Christian Unity

One final factor deserves our attention in this survey of the years leading up to Vatican II: the rise of the ecumenical movement. We have already seen how the word *ecumenical* (whole world) has been used to describe the special authority of Church councils. In the modern period, *ecumenical*—and its companion term *ecumenism*—took on an additional meaning. Today we speak of efforts to heal the divisions within global Christianity as the ecumenical movement.

Christians have long placed a premium on unity. Saint Paul's letters are filled with exhortations to "maintain the unity of the Spirit" (Ephesians 4:3). The Nicene Creed cites unity as one of the marks of the true Church. Our Lord interceded with the Father on behalf of his disciples, present and future, "that they may be one, as we are one" (John 17:22).

The real-life experience of Christianity, however, has always been marred by discord. Episodes in the dark history of disunion include the Great Schism (1054), which split Christian civilization into Eastern and Western factions, the Great Western Schism (1378–1417), which saw three different "popes" claiming the throne of Peter, and the Reformation, which spawned an ever-increasing number of sects.

Two councils in the Middle Ages made progress toward reconciliation with the East. The Council of Constance (1414–1418) successfully resolved the crisis of rival papacies. The Church even offered Protestants safe passage to Trent. From that point on, though, Catholic-Protestant relations deteriorated. First came brutal wars, then chronic theological conflict. Seminaries on both sides trained candidates in the art of polemics (attacking false religion). Protestants valued doctrine over unity. Catholics recognized only one solution to disunity: "return to Rome."

Signs of change appeared as the twentieth century dawned. References to "separated brethren" in papal encyclicals established unity as a standard feature of modern magisterial teaching. An annual Week of Prayer for Christian Unity, initiated by a Franciscan order in the Episcopal tradition, gave reunion a symbolic place in the liturgical calendar. Protestant missionaries raised awareness about unity for practical reasons. Denominational competition in Asia and Africa convinced them that evangelization without ecumenism contradicts the will of Christ. "That the world may believe" can never be divorced from "that they may all be one" (John 17:21).

Modern ecumenism stems from this spirit of missionary cooperation. A major Protestant conference in 1910 sparked a series of international gatherings that led to the founding of the World Council of Churches in 1948. Catholics contributed to the movement in various ways. Desire-Joseph Cardinal Mercier and priest-professors Yves Congar and Johannes Willebrands created networks for dialogue and published Catholicism's earliest theologies of ecumenism. Trappist nun Blessed Maria Gabriella emphasized the spiritual side of ecumenism. The Vatican cautiously supported behind-the-scenes efforts but strongly warned against compromising the fundamentals of the faith.

Pius XII authorized guidelines for Catholic ecumenical engagement in 1948, making unity a permanent item on the Church's modern agenda. A little more than a decade later, though the news of the upcoming Second Vatican Council caught many by surprise, the timing of the announcement made perfect sense. John XXIII's call for a new council coincided with the 1959 Week of Prayer for Christian Unity. The new pope, soon to be known as "Good Pope John," made it clear that Vatican II would be an ecumenical council in both senses of the term, ancient and modern. The twentieth-century renewal of Catholicism would go hand in hand with recommitment to Christian unity.

CHAPTER THREE
The Vision of John XXIII

Vatican II was the largest council in the history of the Catholic Church. Thousands of people participated in its planning, execution, and implementation. Millions have felt its impact, including the one billion Catholics alive today. One man, however, is best associated with the full meaning and measure of the council. Under another pontiff, the Church could have held an ecumenical council in the twentieth century. Without Pope John XXIII, it would not have been Vatican II.

The Making of Pope John

Nothing in Pope John's background indicated that he would have any kind of lasting effect on world Christianity. At the time of his birth, everything suggested just the opposite—an unremarkable life defined by the same down-to-earth realities that have shaped the lives of most men in every age: family, farm, faith, and poverty.

The future pope was born in 1881. Named Angelo Giuseppe Roncalli, he was the eldest son in a peasant family working the land in rural northern Italy. The pope's birthplace, a farmhouse dating to the Counter-Reformation, is today a pilgrimage shrine and museum.

Roncalli's first experiences in education were confined to a local one-room schoolhouse and a modest secondary school several miles from home. Conscious of a vocation from childhood, he entered a minor seminary in the nearby city of Bergamo when he was eleven years old. After a year of mandatory service in the Italian army, he continued his studies at the Pontifical Roman Seminary, thanks to a scholarship for students showing academic potential. He earned advanced degrees in theology and canon law, studied under Vatican official Eugenio Pacelli (the future Pius XII), and was ordained a priest in 1904.

During these years, Roncalli began a lifelong practice of private writing. His *Journal of a Soul* is now recognized as a classic of Christian spirituality. The selections in it represent every phase of his multifaceted career, from seminarian to pope. Retreat notes, resolutions, and a "Spiritual Testament" make the work a spiritual autobiography unique in the history of devotional literature. This prayer for the success of Vatican II, written in 1959, gives us a sense of the spiritual compass that guided his life:

> *May this Council produce abundant fruits: may the light and power of the Gospel be more widely diffused in human society; may new vigor be imparted to the Catholic religion and its missionary function; may we all acquire a more profound knowledge of the Church's doctrine and a wholesome increase of Christian morality* (Journal *391*).

Leadership at Home and Abroad

Father Roncalli could have enjoyed a successful ministry as a priest-professor. He organized a student hostel, taught Church history at the seminary level, and published a critical edition of the works of Saint Charles Borromeo, the sixteenth-century Archbishop of Milan and Church reformer. Early in his career, however, Roncalli was singled out for more demanding duties. Saint Paul spoke of leadership as a supernatural *charism* (grace) in the Christian community (1 Corinthians 12:28). Roncalli exercised the gift of administration for nearly a half-century before he became the chief pastor of the universal Church.

Roncalli learned the basics of Church administration as secretary to the Bishop of Bergamo, Giacomo Radini Tedeschi. Bishop Tedeschi's enthusiasm for the social teaching of Leo XIII inspired the young priest to make economic justice and democratic reform guiding themes of his life's work. As president of the Italian branch of the Society for the

Propagation of the Faith, Roncalli supplemented his concern for social issues with a zeal for foreign missions. Another period of military service, this time as hospital orderly and chaplain during World War I, reinforced his convictions about Christian responsibility in the social order.

Roncalli's career turned decisively toward international diplomacy after the war. Ordained an archbishop in 1925, he was appointed the Vatican's apostolic delegate to Bulgaria, a country dominated by the Orthodox Church and troubled by social unrest. He learned the local language and traveled much of the country on horseback. He applied his organizational skills to humanitarian relief and gained valuable experience in ecumenism, disarming skeptical Orthodox leaders with his sincere interest in Christianity's Eastern heritage.

A similar mission took the Vatican delegate to Turkey and Greece. He continued to invest his energies in East-West dialogue and expanded his outreach to include Turkey's Muslim population and its new secular rulers. He even incorporated Turkish into the liturgy. During the Second World War, Roncalli assisted prisoners of war, coordinated food shipments for civilians, and provided immigration certificates and supplies to Jewish refugees fleeing Nazi persecution.

Later, Roncalli drew upon these wartime experiences as he opened a new chapter in Jewish-Christian relations during his papacy. He removed the phrase "perfidious (unbelieving) Jews" from the Good Friday liturgy and famously introduced himself to a delegation of Jewish leaders with an echo of the biblical patriarch's greeting: "I am Joseph, your brother" (see Genesis 45:4). Thanks largely to Pope John, Jewish-Christian dialogue became a priority for the Church during Vatican II.

Paris, Venice, Rome

Paris in the last months of World War II was Archbishop Roncalli's final foreign assignment. As papal nuncio, he was charged with restoring the French Church, dealing with bishops accused of collaboration with the Germans, and monitoring a new missionary experiment that sent "worker-priests" to the nation's unchurched labor force. The Parisian mission gave the future pope many opportunities to establish dialogue with leaders of the emerging secular Europe. Artists, intellectuals, and politicians—many unbelievers—found in him a churchman whose tolerance and integrity communicated the best of Catholic tradition.

Roncalli returned to Italy in 1953. He was enrolled in the College of Cardinals and installed as Patriarchate (Archbishop) of Venice. He embraced the pastoral responsibility and endeavored to be a good shepherd to his flock, Catholics and Communists alike. He upgraded services to the unemployed, renovated the city's historic tomb of Saint Mark the Evangelist, and quietly prepared for retirement.

When Pius XII died in 1958, Cardinal Roncalli made arrangements to attend the conclave in Rome charged with electing the Fisherman's next successor. A visitor to the patriarchal residence reminded him that Giuseppe Sarto (Pius X), another son of peasants, had held the same office a generation earlier. He, too, left Venice for a papal conclave—and never came back.

The New Pope

Angelo Roncalli was elected pope on October 28, 1958. Vatican insiders assumed he would be a transitional pope, giving the Church a rest after the intense papacy of Pius XII. When Roncalli explained his choice of the name John, he noted that popes with that simplest of names tended to have brief pontificates. No one, not even the new pope, imagined that the Church was on the eve of a revolution.

John XXIII brought to the papacy the same gifts and style that had characterized his ministry in education, diplomacy, and administration. His warmth and informality contrasted greatly with the austerity of previous popes. His visits to Roman institutions, including the city's many parishes, effectively retired the image of the pope as "prisoner of the Vatican." On a broader scale, John made the Church even more "catholic," appointing more than forty bishops in Africa and Asia. He was the first pope to address an encyclical to "all men of good will."

The Pope Speaks

The role of the bishop in the Catholic Church is to teach, sanctify, and govern—a reflection of Christ's threefold office as prophet, priest, and prince (*CCC* 436). Pope John took these tasks very seriously. His eight encyclical letters demonstrate how carefully he attended to the teaching responsibility of the universal pastor. They also show us how he prepared the Church and the world for the Second Vatican Council.

Ad Petri Cathedram (1959) communicated the pope's high expectations for the council. The bishops gathered together for the council, he said, "will consider, in particular, the growth of the Catholic faith, the restoration of sound morals among the Christian flock, and appropriate adaptation of Church discipline to the needs and conditions of our times. This event will be a wonderful spectacle of truth, unity, and charity" (61–62).

Sacerdotii Nostri Primordia (1959) championed the nineteenth-century French pastor Saint John Vianney as the model for parish priests facing the challenges of modern life.

Grata Recordatio (1959) focused on spiritual preparation for the council. The pope encouraged the Church's bishops and all the faithful to recite the rosary with the intent "that the forthcoming Ecumenical Council...will add wondrous growth to the universal Church; and that the renewed vigor of all the Christian virtues which We hope this council will produce will also serve as an invitation and incentive to reunion for Our Brethren and children who are separated from this Apostolic See" (20).

Princeps Pastorum (1959) emphasized the need for a new theology of missions in the twentieth century and greater appreciation for the multicultural character of the Church.

Mater et Magistra (1961), John's first major contribution to papal social teaching, addressed the issues of economic justice that dominated the world during the Cold War. "The Church," John said, "is the standard-bearer and herald of a social doctrine which is unquestionably relevant at any moment to man's needs" (218).

Aeterna Dei Sapientia (1961) invited the bishops to remember the legacy of Saint Leo the Great, the pope who contributed so decisively to the success of the Council of Chalcedon, as they continued to work toward making Vatican II "a wonderful spectacle of Catholic unity" (35).

Paenitentiam Agere (1962) turned again to the subject of interior readiness for the council. Prayer and penance, the pope said, would be the best ways to prepare for the new experience. "If everyone does this, each in his own station in life, he will be enabled to play his individual part in making this Second Ecumenical Vatican Council, which is especially concerned with the refurbishing of Christian morality, an outstanding success" (36).

Pacem in Terris (1963), John's second social encyclical and the best-known of all his writings, highlighted the central place of human rights in the Catholic moral vision. Addressed to a universal audience, it delivered a forceful critique of the nuclear arms race and secured the pontiff's reputation as "Good Pope John."

John Calls a Council

The genesis of Vatican II is now a part of Catholic folklore. Pope John began exploring the possibility of a council in the early days of his pontificate. The decisive moment was January 20, 1959, less than three months after his election. On that day, in a conversation with his secretary of state, Domenico Cardinal Tardini, the full-blown idea came to him. "In response to an inner voice that arose from a kind of heavenly inspiration," the pope said, "We felt that the time was ripe for Us to give the Catholic Church and the whole human family the gift of a new ecumenical council" (*Encyclicals* 389).

John publicly revealed his intent to call a council four days later, on the feast of the Conversion of Saint Paul, the conclusion of that year's Week of Prayer for Christian Unity. He broke the news to a small group of cardinals at Rome's Basilica of Saint Paul Outside the Walls. The pope spoke of two "spectacles" in the postwar society that spurred him to action: the growth of materialism and unbelief in the secular world and the rise of a new confidence in the Catholic community. In response to these developments, he declared, he would initiate three major projects during his pontificate: (1) a *synod* (assembly) for the leaders of the diocese of Rome, (2) a revision or updating of the *Code of Canon Law*, and (3) an ecumenical council. The Italian word that the pope chose to characterize the canon law project—*aggiornamento* (updating)—soon became the unofficial motto for the larger project of the council, too.

Pope John formally announced the Church's twenty-first general council on Christmas Day 1961. In his apostolic constitution *Humanae Salutis*, he called upon the entire Catholic world to read the "signs of the times" (Matthew 16:3), pray for a new outpouring of the Spirit, and work for "a better day for the Church and for mankind." Then, he made it all official:

> *And so, after listening to the opinions of the cardinals of the Holy Roman Church upon this matter, by the authority of Our Lord Jesus Christ, of the Holy Apostles Peter and Paul, and Our own, We announce, We proclaim, We convoke, for this coming year of 1962, the second Sacred Ecumenical and universal Council of the Vatican (Encyclicals 387, 393).*

Privately the pope expressed his sense of anticipation this way: "We are now on the slopes of the sacred mountain. May the Lord give us strength to bring everything to a successful conclusion" (*Journal* 326).

Pope John's Opening Speech

Pope John most effectively articulated his vision for Vatican II in his remarks to the bishops on the first day of the council in 1962: October 11(now his feast day). Today we recognize his speech as a valuable summary of the origins and purpose of the Second Vatican Council. It introduces us to the heart and soul of John XXIII.

The Holy Father opened the historic assembly with a reflection on the Catholic faith as both gift and task. Seeing it as gift, he said, reminds us that we must always remember and cherish the past. We must never cease to honor the saints, martyrs, and ordinary faithful who have transmitted the Gospel to us across the centuries, often with great commitment and sometimes at great cost.

The apostolic teaching that we receive, however, is not simply human testimony, much less human opinion. The Church is both human and divine, and its teaching ministry continues the mission of the incarnate word. "Whoever listens to you," Jesus said, "listens to me" (Luke 10:16). The pope especially emphasized the role played by ecumenical councils in this process of magisterial transmission. Viewed with the eyes of faith, these extraordinary events represent the moments when the institutional Church was most receptive to the leadership of the Spirit.

Next, John turned to the present day—and to the future. The task of faith means discerning how to live the gift of the Gospel in our own time. He recognized the problems plaguing modern experience. All the council fathers had firsthand knowledge of violence, injustice, and rapidly changing moral standards. Some of their brother bishops, noticeable by their absence, were at that moment political prisoners behind the Iron Curtain. Apprehension would only be intensified during the years of the council by a series of world events that included the Cuban Missile Crisis, the assassination of President John F. Kennedy, war in Southeast Asia, and the advent of China's nuclear weapon program.

Still, the pope refused to follow the "prophets of gloom" who saw nothing but evil in contemporary society. The modern world, he declared, offered the body of Christ a terrific challenge but also a tremendous opportunity. Thoughtful updating would help the Church perform its task better: "In fact, by bringing herself up to date where required,...the Church will make men, families, and peoples really turn their minds to heavenly things" (Abbott 712).

What was the Second Vatican Council called to do? John defined the main objective of the council as *evangelical* (Gospel-centered) and its basic orientation as pastoral. Proclaim the Gospel to an anxious and confused world, he encouraged the fathers, and do so with the "medicine of mercy" (Abbott 716). Divine revelation never changes, but formulas communicating the mysteries of the faith may need reexamination or revision. New modes of expression may be necessary if the secular world is to encounter Christ and the Church rediscover its calling.

The pope made it clear that Vatican II was to be different from all other councils. It would not solve a particular problem, condemn a new heresy, or define a new dogma. Its aim would be more general: to raise the "torch of religious truth" and show the Church to be the "loving mother of all" (Abbott 716).

Delivering his memorable speech near the tomb of Saint Peter, John encouraged his fellow bishops to see their actions in the full sweep of salvation history. He invited them to recall that storied circle of apostles some 1,900 years earlier who had boldly initiated the Church's conciliar tradition. Those disciples searched for what "seemed good to the Holy Spirit and to us"—and in the process changed the world.

Now, the pope said, it is our turn. We too seek to align the will of the Church with the will of God in light of the needs of our generation:

> *We might say that heaven and earth are united in the holding of the Council—the saints of heaven to protect our work, the faithful of the earth continuing in prayer to the Lord, and you, seconding the inspiration of the Holy Spirit in order that the work of all may correspond to the modern expectations and needs of the various peoples of the world* (Abbott *718).*

The Impact of Pope John

Pope John did not live long enough to see his beloved council come to its conclusion. Cancer claimed his life a few months after Vatican II's first session. He planted, others watered, "but God," as Saint Paul said, "gave the growth" (1 Corinthians 3:6). Written shortly before his death, these words capture the almost mystical connection between his personal spirituality and the council he felt inspired to call: "This bed is an altar. An altar calls for a victim. Here I am ready. I have before me the clear vision of my soul, of my priesthood, of the Council, of the universal Church" (*Encyclicals* 496).

John XXIII's impact on the Church and the world is beyond calculation. His life presents us with a model of a holy and resourceful priest who lived up to his high calling and kept himself open to heavenly influence—"submissive to the impulse and guidance of the Holy Spirit," as the council would put it (*PO* 12). Pope John will always personify for us the essential freedom of the papacy and the spirit of renewal that Vatican II brought into the modern Catholic experience.

Now that we venerate him as Blessed John XXIII, we can even talk about his ongoing impact on our lives—not just through the council that he initiated but through his prayers and intercessions. History recognizes Vatican II as Pope John's council. To the eyes of faith, it is Blessed John's first miracle.

CHAPTER FOUR
The Events of Vatican II

Vatican II was a crucial turning point for the Catholic Church and much of the non-Catholic world. It was a colossal human relations undertaking as well. Few international meetings of any kind have ever matched it in terms of scope or significance.

If you have ever attended a large professional conference, you can imagine the hurdles that had to be overcome by the council organizers. More than 2,500 bishops, abbots, and superiors of religious orders from six continents—along with personal secretaries, invited theologians, guests, and observers—had to secure roundtrip transportation to Rome four years in a row. They needed food, lodging, and daily ground transportation for each of the council's four roughly two-month-long sessions. Jobs ranging from maintenance to hospitality required an expanded Vatican support staff. The nearly endless flow of paper called for an army of clerical assistants.

Saint Peter's had to be outfitted for a purpose that severely taxed its original design. Bleacher-style seating on each side of the structure's main aisle—wired for sound, telephone, and television systems—transformed the church into a cross between a Renaissance basilica and a modern convention center. Meeting rooms of all shapes and sizes provided space for lectures, receptions, and press conferences between the general congregations or daily business meetings. Newly installed espresso bars took the edge off a demanding schedule and allowed the world's bishops to get acquainted with each other.

Logistics was only the beginning. The real challenge entailed determining the council's mission, setting its agenda, and marshaling the Church's resources to take full advantage of this unrepeatable moment in Christian history. Very quickly, Church leaders realized that the success of the council hinged on the issue of communication—among themselves, with the media, with the international Catholic family, with other Christians, and with the world itself.

Preparation for the Council: 1959 to 1962

The preparation for the council started immediately after Pope John's now-legendary conversation with Cardinal Tardini. From the beginning, the pope designed the entire council project to fit the pattern of the liturgical calendar. The four sessions of the council opened and closed on major holy days. The preparatory period was also punctuated by the rhythm of the Church year. Vatican II quickly became associated with the creative and unifying power of the Holy Spirit. Two papal directives laying the groundwork for the council were issued on Pentecost Sunday, the feast celebrating the Spirit's living presence in the Church.

On Pentecost 1959, Pope John started the preparation process by appointing a special commission comprising members of the Roman *Curia*, Vatican administrators who form the pope's cabinet. The commission's job was to gather information and suggestions from Church leaders around the world. It sent questionnaires to thousands of bishops, theologians, canon lawyers, and heads of religious orders, seeking their input on issues that needed to be addressed at the council.

The next Pentecost, the pope established ten preparatory commissions to decide the details of the council's agenda. The commissions focused on subject areas such as theology, missions, and sacraments, and began to generate position papers for the council's consideration. Pope John also created the Secretariat for Promoting Christian Unity. Charged with fostering Catholic ecumenical work, the Secretariat contributed significantly to the council experience. Since Vatican II, it has been renamed the Pontifical Council for Promoting Christian Unity and is today an important division of the Vatican.

The First Session: 1962

Each session of the Second Vatican Council included a staggering amount of business. Hundreds of hours were devoted to speeches, debates, the writing and rewriting of texts, and the process of consensus-building. There was much to do, and the stakes were high.

Vatican II included much pageantry, too. Imagine the procession through Saint Peter's Square: the long line of bishops in full regalia representing the whole of Christendom, along with the Bishop of Rome carried on the *sedia gestatoria*, the portable papal chair. Eastern-rite bishops and Orthodox observers added color and exotic flair. So did the Swiss Guard in battle formation. Every morning, bishops went to confession in Saint Peter's and celebrated Mass before the day's business. The book of the Gospels was enthroned between two candles after the Eucharist. Opening and closing ceremonies often lasted hours. And everything was in Latin—the documents, the liturgies, even the speeches.

The first session began and ended on two Marian holy days: October 11, 1962, the Maternity of the Blessed Virgin Mary, and December 8, 1962, the Immaculate Conception. Between those two feast days, the council fathers came to a profound realization of the great responsibility laid upon them. The bishops surprised veteran Vatican observers by insisting on making their own decisions, not simply following the Curia's guidelines. The session was adjourned after the first working meeting so the bishops could elect representatives from their own body to serve on the council's commissions, the committees charged with composing the council's documents.

The first document released by the council—a "Message to Humanity"—also took many by surprise. In just over 1,000 words, the bishops restated the principal goals of the council and identified the Church's main mission as service to the world "so loved" by God (John 3:16). Renewing the Church and witnessing to the Gospel, the fathers declared, meant solidarity with the poor and the defense of human dignity. The message was especially noteworthy for its ecumenical outreach: "We humbly and ardently call for all men to work along with us in building up a more just and brotherly city in this world" (Abbott 6).

For the rest of the first session, the council fathers began their evaluation of the commissions' documents. The bishops discussed the texts line by line. They voted on sketches called *schemata* or *schemas* and then voted on the final versions. Every text required a two-thirds majority approval to become part of magisterial teaching. The council eventually issued sixteen authoritative documents. When we speak of the theology of Vatican II, we think specifically of the theological vision set forth in those sixteen documents.

Three draft documents—on divine revelation, the liturgy, and the Church—were ready for consideration during the first session. The *schema* on revelation exposed the greatest degree of division among the fathers. Many thought its talk of "two sources" of revelation, Scripture and tradition, simply repeated the slogans of the Counter-Reformation and did not take seriously new perspectives in biblical studies. The pope intervened in the debate, reassuring the fathers that disagreement was a healthy sign of freedom in the Church. He directed two committees to work together on a new text and encouraged the fathers to move forward.

Soon it became evident that the council could not complete its work in a single session. Pope John concluded the session on the feast celebrating the mystery of Mary's redemption. He spoke of a "mystic, heavenly rainbow" linking the day with the council's inauguration on the feast of our Lady's motherhood. Weakened by cancer, he still exhibited his characteristic optimism. He commended the bishops for their hard work and encouraged them to prepare for the long road ahead: "Then, doubtless, will dawn that new Pentecost which is the object of our yearning—a Pentecost that will increase the Church's wealth of spiritual strength and extend her maternal influence and saving power to every sphere of human endeavor" (*Encyclicals* 444).

A New Pope

Pope John did live to see one more Pentecost. He died on June 3, 1963, Pentecost Monday. The Church and the world mourned. The Church also wondered what the future had in store. Who will fill the shoes of the Fisherman after this "transitional" pope? What will the new pope do about the unfinished council? How and when will the council come to its conclusion?

Some questions were answered on June 21. The papal conclave elected Giovanni Battista Cardinal Montini, a figure highly respected in Catholic leadership circles. He was longtime pro-secretary of state under Pius XII and Archbishop of Milan for nearly a decade, well-known for his interest in social reform. As Pope Paul VI, he made it clear that Vatican II would be the top priority of his papacy. His first encyclical used John's word, *aggiornamento* (updating), to communicate the aim of his own pontificate. The son of a lawyer-editor, Paul brought to the papacy the administrator's attention to detail and the diplomat's appreciation of dialogue.

The Second Session: 1963

Pope Paul convened Vatican II's second session on September 29, 1963, the feast of Saint Michael the Archangel. Like John, he, too, delivered an opening address to set the tone for the meeting. Now the bishops were seasoned council fathers, more sensitive to the details of parliamentary process, more aware of the issues at stake, and more realistic about how long it might take to complete their task. Paul took these facts into account as he reacquainted the assembly with its lofty assignment.

The new pope also clarified what some had thought too vague during the first session. He identified four key goals for the council: (1) reexamination of the nature of the Church, (2) renewal of the Church's self-awareness, (3) advocacy of Christian unity, and (4) promotion of dialogue with the contemporary world. Above all, he said, the council must present Christ as the answer to the questions of the modern age: "Christ who is both the road we travel and our guide on the way" (*Council Speeches* 19–20).

The second session's work revolved around the *schema* on the Church. Discussion became heated as the bishops tackled issues dealing with the offices and ministries of the Church. Two topics in particular occupied the fathers.

The first was the *collegiality* of bishops—the mutual respect for and common work of the apostles' successors. The individual bishop's authority in his own diocese is one thing, but what about his connection with his colleagues? What about the authority of the *college*, or brotherhood, of bishops as a whole? The issue revived old questions about the relationship between bishops and councils, on the one hand, and the papacy, on the other.

The second topic was the proposal to reestablish the institution of the permanent *diaconate* (ministry of deacons). In the early Church, deacons occupied a distinct position of service, not a transitional step toward priesthood. What made the idea especially controversial at the council was the proposal to ordain married men to the office (see 1 Timothy 3:12).

The council moderators, supported by the pope, intervened into the council program when these issues threatened to hinder the progress of the session. The fathers were polled on several points concerning the ministry of bishops and deacons. The results indicated that the document on the Church needed much more work and the fathers much more time to bring the debate to a satisfactory resolution.

By the beginning of Advent, everyone realized that Vatican II would continue for at least one more session. A welcomed sign of success was the council's approval of two completed documents: the Constitution on the Sacred Liturgy and the Decree on the Instruments of Social Communication. Statements on more sensitive issues such as ecumenism, religious liberty, and the Jews would have to wait for another day.

Pope Paul concluded the session on December 4, the feast of Saint Peter Chrysologus, doctor of the Church, and Saint Barbara, virgin and martyr. He publicly embraced the ideal of collegiality, referring to himself simply as "Paul, Bishop of the Catholic Church." The high point of the ceremony was the pope's announcement of his plan to visit the Holy Land after Christmas. Along with future trips to south

Asia, the Americas, Africa, and Australia, this papal pilgrimage vividly reinforced Vatican II's message about a new attitude of openness toward the world.

The Pope Between Sessions

Paul's journey to the Holy Land was an overwhelming success. It conveyed on the world's stage the core values of the council. The pope's cordial meeting in Jerusalem with Eastern Orthodox leader Athenagoras, Patriarch of Constantinople, did more for ecumenism in one symbolic stroke than all the meetings and manifestos had ever accomplished.

Paul's first encyclical, *Ecclesiam Suam* (1964), also advanced council themes. Its image of four concentric circles of dialogue—with the world, with non-Christian religions, with non-Catholic Christians, and within the Catholic community itself—established dialogue as a permanent fixture of magisterial thought. "Our dialogue," the pope said, "should be as universal as we can make it" (76). Paul's founding of the Vatican Secretariat for Non-Christians, later renamed the Pontifical Council for Interreligious Dialogue, launched the Church into the uncharted waters of interfaith encounter.

The Third Session: 1964

The council's third session began with a bold liturgical gesture. The pope and twenty-four bishops *concelebrated* Mass—presiding together as equals at the altar. It was September 14, 1964, the Exaltation of the Holy Cross. Dialogue, collegiality, and liturgical renewal were now no longer just abstract ideas.

After the ceremony, the bishops faced their fullest agenda yet. A backlog of *schemas* demanded a more rapid pace of deliberation. Three finished documents were approved during the session: the Decree on Eastern Catholic Churches (Eastern-rite Churches in communion with Rome), the Decree on Ecumenism, and the Constitution on the Church. The ideas expressed in these texts, especially references to the Church as the "People of God," profoundly influenced the emerging theological outlook of the other documents still in committee.

A slate of new *schemas* submitted to the fathers addressed all sorts of topics: the reform of religious life, the formation of priests, the ministry of bishops, the vocation of the laity, missionary work, and Christian education. Proposed declarations on religious freedom and the Church's relationship to Jews and non-Christians exposed deep divisions among the bishops. Critics of the religious liberty text thought it contradicted previous Church teaching on Church-state matters. Bishops from the Middle East feared that an overly positive statement on Judaism would endanger Catholics in Arab lands.

A new document called "*Schema* 13" also stimulated debate. It covered a broad array of subjects dealing with modern life—from marriage and economics to nuclear war and atheism. Eventually it would become the Pastoral Constitution on the Church in the Modern World, one of the best-known publications of the council.

By far, the most important text that returned to the assembly during the third session was the previously tabled document on divine revelation. As it evolved through one revision after another, it placed more and more emphasis on the importance of biblical studies in Catholic theology and the central place of the Bible in Catholic spirituality.

All the drama was not in the business of the council, though. The assembly heard its first lay speaker, women were invited to join an expanding circle of auditors, and daily worship showcased the Church's liturgical diversity. On one occasion, the fathers celebrated Mass according to the Coptic (ancient Egyptian) rite.

Pope Paul played an increasingly prominent role as the session proceeded. He directly intervened in council affairs—by letter (on bishops and papal primacy) and in person (on the Church's missionary mandate). He postponed a vote on the religious liberty document, fearing the escalation of conflict, and appointed a special commission to review the question of artificial birth control—an issue recently revived due to the invention of "the pill." Committed to the council's call to reclaim the simplicity of the Gospel, he placed his silver tiara on the altar of Saint Peter's and never again wore the famous "triple crown."

Vatican II's strenuous third session came to an end on November 21, the feast of the Presentation of Mary in the Temple. Pope Paul praised the work of the fathers and took the opportunity to bestow upon the

Blessed Virgin a new title: *Mater Ecclesiae*, "Mother of the Church" (see *CCC* 963). The session ended as it began—with a concelebrated Mass. This time the pope officiated with twenty-four bishops whose dioceses around the world housed popular shrines dedicated to Mary.

The Final Session: 1965

During the intersession period, the Church was still bustling with activity. Bishops and council theologians raced against the clock to complete all the documents scheduled for the fourth session's heavy agenda. Priests, religious, and laypeople across the globe scrambled to stay up to date on the latest from Rome.

Pope Paul was especially busy. He made a historic missionary journey to India. He issued two new encyclicals (on prayer for peace and the Eucharist). He established a new Vatican department to promote dialogue with atheists: the Secretariat for Non-Believers.

Vatican II's fourth session was its longest, its most productive, and its last. The Exaltation of the Cross (September 14) and the feast of the Immaculate Conception (December 8) served as bookends for the council's closing act. The session's ceremony, like its workload, was at peak level. Something as simple as the pope's decision to enter Saint Peter's on foot, leaving behind the *sedia gestatoria*, powerfully communicated a spirit of new beginnings.

Paul's contributions to the final session shaped the course of discussion on the council floor and the outcome of the council as a whole. He endorsed the idea of a synod of bishops meeting regularly after the council and committed himself to the reform of the Roman Curia. He also started the process that would lead to the beatification of his predecessors, Pius XII and John XXIII. His October trip to the United States, featuring a speech before the United Nations and a Mass at Yankee Stadium, greatly boosted international interest in the council.

Most of the fourth session was devoted to the final debates and final votes on the remaining texts. The fathers approved a total of eleven documents: six *decrees* on the ministry of bishops, the renewal of religious life, the training of priests, the ministry of priests, the lay apostolate, and the Church's missionary activity; three *declarations* on education, religious freedom, and world religions; and two *constitutions*: the Dogmatic Constitution on Divine Revelation and the revised version of "*Schema* 13," the Pastoral Constitution on the Church in the Modern World.

Three of these eleven documents received a significant number of negative votes: seventy against the religious freedom declaration, seventy-five against the Church in the Modern World, and eighty-eight against the statement on non-Christian religions. Today we realize that these "no" votes were warning signs of stormy seas ahead. At the time, however, eagerness to put Vatican II's message into action outweighed any uneasiness about the future of renewal in the Church.

The Close of the Council

After seven years, counting the planning phase and the four working sessions, the Second Vatican Council came to its conclusion as the Church entered another Advent season. Long processions lined Saint Peter's Square, and pilgrims poured into the Eternal City. Three days were set aside for the final ceremonies.

On December 4, again the feast of Saints Peter Chrysologus and Barbara, the bishops and non-Catholic observers met for a first-ever ecumenical service at the place where Pope John had started it all: Saint Paul's Outside the Walls. The program included prayers, hymns, Scripture lessons, and an address by the pope. Paul concluded his remarks with the story of Vladimir Soloviev, the Russian philosopher who once spent a sleepless night in a dark monastic corridor searching until sunrise for the door to his cell—the perfect parable, the pope suggested, for Christian disciples in a new ecumenical age.

The feast of Saint Ambrose, December 7, brought another unparalleled ecumenical event. Pope Paul and Patriarch Athenagoras—at coordinated proceedings in Rome and Istanbul—simultaneously lifted the sentences of excommunication that had separated their Churches since the East-West Schism of 1054. In a joint statement, the two leaders expressed their hope that the gesture of reconciliation would lead all Christians to rediscover the communion of faith and charity that characterized the Christian movement during its first thousand years.

Thunderous applause erupted in Saint Peter's when Paul and the Patriarch's delegate greeted each other with the kiss of peace.

In his homily for the day, Pope Paul reminded the assembly just how unusual Vatican II's orientation had been. Never before had a council focused so intently on the nature and mission of the Church, and never before had a council concentrated so generously on the human experience. "Yes, the Church of the council has been concerned," he said, "not just with herself and with her relationship of union with God, but with man—man as he really is today" (*Address*, paragraph 11).

The next day, December 8, the feast of the Immaculate Conception, the final ceremony was held outdoors. Thousands crowded the piazza of Saint Peter's. Thousands more followed the events on radio and television. The pontiff's homily at Mass placed the council in the broadest possible context: "From this Catholic center of Rome, no one, in principle, is unreachable; in principle, all men can and must be reached. For the Catholic Church, no one is a stranger" (*Homily*, paragraph 4).

After Mass, selected cardinals read special messages to specific groups of people around the world: rulers, intellectuals, artists, women, workers, the poor, the sick, and youth. The message to young people communicated what many were already calling the "spirit" of Vatican II:

*Rich with a long past ever living in her, and marching on toward human perfection in time and the ultimate destinies of history and of life, the Church is the real youth of the world. She possesses what constitutes the strength and the charm of youth, that is to say, the ability to rejoice with what is beginning, to give oneself unreservedly, to renew oneself and to set out again for new conquests. Look upon the Church and you will find in her the face of Christ, the genuine, humble, and wise Hero, the Prophet of truth and love, the Companion and Friend of youth (*Abbott 737*).

CHAPTER FIVE
The People of Vatican II

No one knows exactly how many people participated in the Second Vatican Council. One estimate places the number as high as 7,500—counting all Church leaders, assistants, advisors, observers, guests, media representatives, support staff, and even acolytes and choirboys. Getting a mental picture of the full spectrum of participants gives us a better sense of the scope and richness of the Vatican II experience.

Some participants were always in the spotlight. They played high-profile roles in the daily general congregations and the council's ceremonial life. They made speeches, presided over meetings, interacted with the media, and celebrated the Church's unending "sacrifice of praise" (Hebrews 13:15) at a pivotal moment in their tradition's history.

Others worked behind the scenes. Modern "co-workers with the truth" (3 John 8), they researched disputed questions, composed documents, edited texts, and initiated dialogue across boundaries of culture, language, and creed. Their names may be remembered today only by professional historians, but their words are permanently enshrined in the teachings of Vatican II. Thanks to them, phrases such as the "People of God," the "universal call to holiness," the "universal sacrament of salvation," and the "source and summit of the Christian life" are now standard features of the way we conceive and communicate our faith. Echoed in everything from papal encyclicals to Sunday homilies, their words have forever changed the way Catholicism sounds inside and outside the Church.

Popes at the Council

As we have seen, two popes left an indelible mark on the council. John gave the meeting its overarching pastoral orientation. His theme of *aggiornamento* still governs the way we think of the council and its legacy. Aside from his leadership in the opening and closing ceremonies, however, Pope John did not take part in the day-to-day business of the council. He viewed the proceedings on closed-circuit television and intervened in the deliberations only once—during the debate on revelation.

Paul, who participated in the first session as Cardinal Montini, fine-tuned the self-understanding of Vatican II, describing it as a uniquely Church-centered council. He monitored the council's progress by analyzing each new draft document with a small team of advisors. He entered the decision-making process more than John did, but still only when certain issues called for special attention—issues such as collegiality and contraception. Pope Paul had the additional responsibility of overseeing the Church after 1965, as the council's decrees were transformed into policy and practice in every diocese and religious order around the world.

Future Popes
at the Council

John and Paul, however, were not the only popes at Vatican II. Three future popes were there, too. Albino Luciani, bishop of northeast Italy's Vittorio Veneto and later Patriarch of Venice, attended all four sessions. In 1978, he succeeded Pope Paul and became Pope John Paul, honoring the pontiffs of the council with the first double name in papal history.

Karol Wojtyla, later John Paul II, also participated in the council—in the first two sessions as Krakow's auxiliary bishop and in the third and fourth as its archbishop. His speeches on religious freedom and his work on the commission crafting "*Schema* 13" made a lasting impression on the assembly and on Pope Paul. Wojtyla, now venerated as Blessed John Paul II, was the only bishop to address his remarks to "brothers and sisters," acknowledging the presence of women in the audience.

His book *Sources of Renewal: The Implementation of the Second Vatican Council*, published before he was pope, shows how deeply the experience shaped his spirituality. As pope, he often spoke of the council as the Holy Spirit's gift to the Church.

Joseph Ratzinger, the future Pope Benedict XVI, participated as one of the leading theological advisors at the council. A young university professor accompanying the Archbishop of Cologne, Father Ratzinger quickly rose to prominence at the council. The Constitution on Divine Revelation, the Constitution on the Church, the Constitution on the Church in the Modern World, and the Decree on the Church's Missionary Activity bear traces of his outlook and learning. After the council, especially as head of the Vatican's Congregation for the Doctrine of the Faith (CDF), Ratzinger became one of the world's preeminent interpreters of the council's message. His book *Theological Highlights of Vatican II* sparked a career-long endeavor to assess its strengths, weaknesses, and long-term meaning. John Paul II called him the "ultimate theologian of the council" (Oder 82).

Bishops and Cardinals

Popes were not the only leading actors at the council. Without the world's bishops and cardinals, there would have been no Vatican II. Hundreds of churchmen from scores of countries participated in the life-changing event. In recent years, most of these princes of the Church have passed from the scene. Many left behind memoirs, granting us valuable insights into this remarkable episode in Christian history. Today the structures and programs in any given diocese across the world tell the story of one bishop's effort to transplant Vatican II into a particular cultural context. Together these successors of the apostles represent the modern Church's "greatest generation."

A handful of fathers stand out because of the uniqueness of their role or the exceptional quality of their achievement at the council. The Italian Alfredo Cardinal Ottaviani was a force to be reckoned with because of his powerful position in the Curia. A longtime Vatican administrator, he was now head of the Holy Office (today's CDF), the department responsible for the defense of orthodox teaching. He urged caution as the fathers considered liturgical reform and warned against uncritical acceptance of new ideas. He thought the council should be more assertive in reaffirming traditional Catholic claims and more aggressive in confronting contemporary challenges such as Communism.

German-born Augustin Cardinal Bea was instrumental in shaping the council's approach to ecumenical and interfaith affairs. He was a prolific Old Testament scholar, a member of the Society of Jesus, a pioneer in Jewish-Catholic relations, and a trusted associate of Pius XII. Pope John appointed him the founding director of the Secretariat for Christian Unity. Bea enthusiastically backed the idea of inviting non-Catholic representatives to observe the meeting. During the council, he served as their host. He also worked closely with the commissions revising the statements on revelation, religious liberty, ecumenism, and non-Christian religions.

The Belgian cardinal, Leon Joseph Suenens, was a bold champion of reform at the council. One of the most effective moderators of the assembly, he helped to bring order and focus to the sometimes unruly program. When Pope Paul invited lay leaders to attend the sessions, Suenens argued for the inclusion of women. The cardinal spoke at the council on the Spirit in the Church and advocated a review of teaching on marriage and birth control. After Vatican II, he served as unofficial patron for the Catholic charismatic movement, the innovative movement emphasizing supernatural gifts in the Christian life.

Maximos IV Cardinal Saigh, Patriarch of the Melkite Church of Antioch, personified the cultural and liturgical diversity within Catholic Christianity. He refused to deliver his speeches in Latin (speaking in French instead), and he reminded his brothers that married clergy and the liturgical use of local languages were venerable traditions of the Eastern-rite experience. Fearing an anti-Christian Muslim backlash, he also objected to an overly favorable statement regarding Jews.

Other influential bishops included Germany's Frings, Chile's Henriquez, Austria's Konig, France's Lienart, Canada's Leger, and the Italians Lercaro, Ruffini, and Siri. In the U.S. delegation we find names still familiar to American Catholics: Alter (Cincinnati), Cushing

(Boston), Deardon (Detroit), Meyer (Chicago), Ritter (St. Louis), and Spellman (New York).

One final example, Francis Arinze, represents the new class of leaders for whom Vatican II was, in effect, a moment of personal and professional formation. A native of Nigeria and a convert to Christianity, he was the youngest bishop at the council. Today, he is a senior churchman with an impressive record in the Curia's global ministry—eighteen years as director of the Pontifical Council for Interreligious Dialogue and twelve as head of the Congregation for Divine Worship and the Discipline of the Sacraments. Like other bishops in his generation, Cardinal Arinze has spent his entire career advancing the values of Vatican II.

Major Theologians

The presence of invited theologians—more than 400 of the Church's best minds—gave the atmosphere of John's pastoral council an unusually academic feel. Some were appointed by the pope. Most were appointed by local bishops. They came from universities and seminaries all around the world. Called *periti* (expert advisors), they made Vatican II an unparalleled moment in Catholic intellectual history.

The *periti* served the council fathers as consultants and writers but did not address the assembly or vote. Their influence was felt most fully in the commission meetings and the many informal discussions. Their lectures and publications had a tremendous impact on the assembly's evolving sense of identity and purpose.

The roll of the *periti* reads like a "Who's Who" of twentieth-century Catholic theology. The "new theologians" Congar, de Lubac, and Danielou emerged as key leaders, as did Ratzinger, the Swiss priest Hans Kung, and the Germans Bernard Haring and Karl Rahner. Marie-Dominique Chenu and his fellow Dominican Edward Schillebeeckx were also active in Rome during the council years but were never technically *periti*. Among the Americans, two *periti* were especially noteworthy: Jesuit moral theologian John Courtney Murray, the principal architect of the council's argument for religious liberty, and Redemptorist priest Francis Xavier Murphy, whose *Letters From Vatican City*, published under the pen name Xavier Rynne, shaped public opinion more than any other eyewitness report.

Non-Catholic Observers

For many council fathers and *periti*, daily interaction with non-Catholic Christians was one of the most rewarding features of Vatican II. Serious and sustained theological dialogue with "separated brethren" was still a new and uncertain venture. The participation of clergy from non-Catholic traditions turned the twenty-first general council into the first truly *ecumenical* council in Catholic history.

Authorities from Armenian, Coptic, Ethiopian, Syrian, and Russian traditions brought the Orthodox East to the council. Mainline Protestantism was represented by leaders from a variety of communions—Anglican, Congregational, Disciples of Christ, Lutheran, Methodist, Quaker, Reformed (Presbyterian), Unitarian (liberal Christian), and the World Council of Churches.

The Vatican called the invited guests observers. Many of them were distinguished churchmen and scholars already active in ecumenical circles. The observers attended the general congregations, participated in unofficial discussions, received regular briefings from Cardinal Bea, and offered commentary on the council's documents and decisions. They did not, however, vote or play any official role in the decision-making process.

Thirty-nine observers participated in the first session. More than 100 would be involved by the end of the council. Their published accounts of their experiences—such as Robert McAfee Brown's *Observer in Rome* and Albert Outler's *Methodist Observer at Vatican II*—are cherished today as models of ecumenical outreach and theological reflection.

Jewish leaders also followed the council closely, though none was an official observer. Rabbi Abraham Joshua Heschel, an authority on Hebrew prophecy, represented the American Jewish Committee in its communication with the Vatican. Along with his colleagues, many of whom had lost loved ones in the Holocaust, Heschel urged the Church to condemn anti-Semitism, abandon its mission to the Jews, and renounce the charge of deicide (God-killing). He met with Cardinal Bea and was granted a private audience with Pope Paul, who later quoted Heschel in one of his addresses—a first in papal history. Though the council's declaration on Judaism fell short of Jewish expectations, the worldwide Jewish community still greeted Vatican II as a major step toward healing a long-troubled relationship.

Auditors and the Media

Two other important groups at Vatican II were the auditors and the media representatives. The auditors were leading laymen and religious sisters invited to observe and in a few cases address the assembly. Laywomen joined the auditors after the second session. A total of fifty-two auditors participated in the council. Some served as advisors for the commissions. Sister Mary Luke Tobin, head of the Sisters of Loretto, worked on the commissions planning "*Schema* 13" and the document on lay ministry. Numerous other women participated in unofficial council activities. Dorothy Day, editor of *The Catholic Worker* newspaper, met with bishops and *periti*, arguing for a more robust witness to peace in the council proclamations.

Journalists covered the council from the beginning. The Vatican's public relations policy began with unrealistic assumptions about confidentiality. After the first session, the council press office adopted more pragmatic measures. Coordinated by bishops and *periti*, it distributed daily bulletins and scheduled regular briefings and press conferences for different language groups. The U.S. bishops organized their own press panel to accommodate American news agencies. During the fourth session, Pope Paul received around 500 reporters in a special audience, and council organizers sponsored a special photography exhibition celebrating the personalities and events of the council in pictures.

The Council's "Absent Fathers"

Some of the people whose influence was most keenly felt at Vatican II were not physically present at the meeting. We call these unseen figures the council's "absent fathers."

One was John Henry Newman. His concept of the development of doctrine gained widespread acceptance during the council years. The Dogmatic Constitution on Divine Revelation reflects his understanding of the dynamism of the Church's faith, ever growing and expanding, always aiming toward the fullness of truth:

The Tradition that comes from the apostles makes progress in the Church, with the help of the Holy Spirit. There is a growth in insight into the realities and words that are being passed on.... Thus, as the centuries go by, the Church is always advancing towards the plenitude of divine truth, until eventually the words of God are fulfilled in her (DV 8).

Another "absent father" was the Jesuit priest and paleontologist Pierre Teilhard de Chardin, famous in scientific circles for his study of Peking Man. His original theory of evolution and the Incarnation leading the universe to God, the "Omega Point," is echoed in the Pastoral Constitution on the Church in the Modern World:

The Word of God, through whom all things were made, was made flesh, so that as a perfect man he could save all men and sum up all things in himself. The Lord is the goal of human history, the focal point of the desires of history and civilization, the center of mankind, the joy of all hearts, and the fulfillment of all aspirations....Animated and drawn together in his Spirit we press onwards on our journey towards the consummation of history which fully corresponds to the plan of his love: "to unite all things in him, things in heaven and things on earth" (Ephesians 1:10) (GS 45).

Philosopher Jacques Maritain also had an impact on the mind of the council. France's ambassador to the Vatican after World War II, he left a deep impression on the future Paul VI, who later cited the Frenchman's work in his encyclical *Populorum Progressio* (1967). Maritain's attempt to reconcile Catholic tradition and modern democracy informed the teaching on human rights in the Declaration on Religious Freedom and the vision of a "new humanism" in the Pastoral Constitution on the Church in the Modern World (*GS* 55).

Vatican II becomes all the more remarkable when we realize that two of its "absent fathers" were Jewish. Historian Jules Isaac's criticism of anti-Jewish tendencies in Christianity set the background for the Declaration on Non-Christian Religions. Martin Buber's philosophy of dialogue, articulated in his classic *I and Thou* (1923), helped make "dialogue with the world and with men of all shades of opinion" (*GS* 43) one of the council's signature themes.

CHAPTER SIX
The Message of Vatican II

All who participated in the Second Vatican Council marveled at its phenomenal human dimension. The inspiring encounter with fellow Christians across vast cultural, racial, language, and theological barriers made Vatican II one of the greatest people events of the twentieth century. In the end, though, the council was about *ideas* expressed in words written on paper—all told anywhere from 500 to 700 pages of paper in a standard collection.

Sixteen documents were written, debated, and approved during the four sessions. Those documents, like the decisions from the other twenty ecumenical councils, are now part of the Church's magisterial teaching. They are quoted in the catechism, papal encyclicals, and countless theological and devotional publications. They reverberate daily in our prayer and worship. Some passages rival the best of the Christian literary heritage for their beauty and the force of their wisdom. The documents are the message and voice of Vatican II.

Paul VI spoke of Vatican II as the most Church-centered council in history. As we have seen, it did not concentrate on the narrow problem of a new heresy or schism. Vatican II trained its sights on the broader question—and the uniquely modern question—of how to live the Gospel in an era of social change. The council's documents present us with a portrait of the Church at a crossroads, a moment of collective soul-searching and intentional recommitment. In their pages, we see the body of Christ, enlivened by worship, renewing its identity and reclaiming its apostolic mission to serve "the world God has so loved as to give his only begotten Son for it" (*PO* 22).

Vatican II's
Sixteen Documents

The sixteen documents are divided into three categories, and each has an official Latin title.

Four documents are called constitutions:
- Constitution on the Sacred Liturgy *(Sacrosanctum Concilium),*
- Dogmatic Constitution on the Church *(Lumen Gentium,* also called *De Ecclesia*),
- Dogmatic Constitution on Divine Revelation *(Dei Verbum),*
- Pastoral Constitution on the Church in the Modern World *(Gaudium et Spes).*

Nine are decrees:
- Decree on the Apostolate of the Laity *(Apostolicam Actuositatem),*
- Decree on Eastern Catholic Churches *(Orientalium Ecclesiarum),*
- Decree on the Church's Missionary Activity *(Ad Gentes),*
- Decree on Ecumenism *(Unitatis Redintegratio),*
- Decree on the Instruments of Social Communication *(Inter Mirifica),*
- Decree on the Ministry and Life of Priests *(Presbyterorum Ordinis),*
- Decree on the Bishops' Pastoral Office in the Church *(Christus Dominus),*
- Decree on Priestly Formation *(Optatam Totius),*
- Decree on the Appropriate Renewal of the Religious Life *(Perfectae Caritatis).*

Three are declarations:

- Declaration on Christian Education *(Gravissimum Educationis),*
- Declaration on the Relationship of the Church to Non-Christian Religions *(Nostra Aetate),*
- Declaration on Religious Freedom *(Dignitatis Humanae).*

Constitution on the Sacred Liturgy

The Constitution on the Sacred Liturgy was the first official document approved by Vatican II. Its opening statement gives us the council's first articulation of its objectives: "The sacred council has set out to impart an ever-increasing vigor to the Christian life of the faithful; to adapt more closely to the needs of our age those institutions which are subject to change; to foster whatever can promote union among all who believe in Christ; to strengthen whatever can help call all mankind into the Church's fold" (*SC* 1).

When it comes specifically to liturgical matters, the text surprises us. For many people, Vatican II means only one thing: dramatic change in worship. Some even imagine that the council was called for the purpose of rejecting the liturgical past. We forget that the Tridentine Mass, revised by Pope John, was the official rite celebrated during the council itself.

What we find in the constitution is not hostility toward the Church's heritage but rather a hymn to the riches of sacramental worship. The liturgy is hailed as "the summit toward which the activity of the Church is directed...[and] the fount from which all her power flows" (10). The Eucharist deserves special honor as the supreme source of divine grace.

The document calls for a "general restoration" of the liturgy in light of the conditions of contemporary culture (21), but it keeps its recommendations on the level of basic principles. Liturgy should be simple, clear, and reverent. It should especially promote "full, conscious, and active participation" on the part of the people and greater appreciation for the "treasures of the Bible" (14, 51). Local languages and modern art may be introduced as needed. Still, Latin "is to be preserved" (36),

Gregorian chant given "pride of place" (116), and the pipe organ "held in high esteem" (120).

The overall tone of the constitution is informed by respect for tradition and openness to modern conditions—*ressourcement* (return to the sources) and *aggiornamento* (updating) at the same time. Some things can be changed; others are divinely established. "There must be no innovations unless the good of the Church genuinely and certainly requires them, and care must be taken that any new forms adopted should in some way grow organically from forms already existing" (23). The liturgical changes most often associated with Vatican II were not specifically mandated by the council but gradually entered Catholic life during the postconciliar period.

Dogmatic Constitution on the Church

The Dogmatic Constitution on the Church builds on the document on the liturgy. It continues the eucharistic theme, describing the Church as a "sign and instrument...of communion with God and of unity among men" (*LG* 1). The Church is the "universal sacrament of salvation" (48).

In the sacraments, we use ordinary things such as bread, water, wine, and oil to help us discover the extraordinary presence of God in our lives. Catholicism's sacramental principle, however, goes far beyond the Church's standard seven rites. It sees all of creation as potentially a vehicle for God's saving grace. The Dogmatic Constitution on the Church declares the Church itself to be one immense sacrament—a cosmic body of millions of human beings, transmitting grace to the world as it spans the globe and the gap between the living and the dead.

The constitution uses many other images to capture the mystery of the Church. Two that sparked great enthusiasm in the years following the council are the "People of God" and the "Pilgrim Church." Both express the human, unfinished character of Christian experience, and both underscore the dignity of the "common priesthood of the faithful" (10).

The document also describes the Church as an ordered community. *Hierarchy* (from the Greek for "holy rule") is not an optional or man-made component of the Church's identity. All the structures of authority—including papal primacy, apostolic succession, ranks of ministry, and the college of bishops—are permanently built into the Church's makeup by divine design.

The most striking claims of the constitution concern the Church's uniqueness and its inclusive relationship with non-Christian religions. Christ founded one Church, the "pillar and bulwark of the truth" (1 Timothy 3:15). "This Church," the document states, "subsists in the Catholic Church, which is governed by the successor of Peter and by the bishops in communion with him" (8). Holiness and truth, however, can be found outside the visible Church and outside of Christianity. Jews, Muslims, and those who seek "an unknown God" (Acts 17:23) are mysteriously related to the body of baptized disciples. Salvation is possible for those "who, through no fault of their own, do not know the Gospel of Christ or his Church, but who nevertheless seek God with a sincere heart, and, moved by grace, try in their actions to do his will as they know it through the dictates of their conscience" (16).

Dogmatic Constitution on Divine Revelation

The Dogmatic Constitution on Divine Revelation celebrates the indispensable role of divine light in the Christian life. Because of revelation, we can see the truth about God and the truth about ourselves. In an age that questioned the existence of God, Vatican II affirmed not only belief in God but belief in a God who communicates—who spoke long ago to prophets (Hebrews 1:1), and who speaks to us today through his "living and active" word (Hebrews 4:12).

The council fathers wanted to avoid a static approach to revelation. Their debate over the document reminds us of how supremely Catholic the word "both" is. In its simple way, this little word captures the genius and generosity of the Catholic world view. We speak, for example, of God as both one and three, Christ as both human and divine, Mary as both virgin and mother, the Eucharist as both bread and flesh, the Church as both earthly and heavenly, and ourselves as both saints and sinners. The Dogmatic Constitution on Divine Revelation speaks of God's communication with the world in this same distinctively Catholic way.

We know God through both natural reason and supernatural revelation. Revelation is both the divine communication of saving truths (doctrine) and the self-revelation of truth itself (God). Revelation is transmitted through both the teaching of appointed leaders (tradition) and the words of inspired writings (Scripture). The Bible is both God's word about humanity and humanity's word about God. It is both an ancient book tied to Near Eastern cultures and eternal wisdom relevant to everyone. It makes "the voice of the Holy Spirit sound again and again" (*DV* 21).

When we noted Newman's influence on the council, we saw how the constitution adopted the idea of doctrinal development. Another important element in this dynamic view of revelation is the part played by the Church's teaching office. Christ gave the apostles the right to "bind" and "loose" (Matthew 18:18) and the Spirit to guide them "into all the truth" (John 16:13). Revelation, then, has divinely appointed interpreters. Tradition, Scripture, and the magisterium "are so connected and associated that one of them cannot stand without the others" (10).

Most of all, the constitution aims at recentering the Bible in Catholic life. Modern study of the text is encouraged, and Scripture is recognized as the "soul" of theology (24). At the same time, traditional features of doctrine are reaffirmed: the divine authorship of Scripture, the unity of the Old and New Testaments, and the Bible's accuracy about what Jesus "really did and taught" (19). Scripture "firmly, faithfully and without error" teaches the truth necessary for salvation (11).

All of which matters little, though, if Scripture is divorced from spirituality. Saint Jerome's maxim about ignorance of Scripture and ignorance of Christ is more than an invitation to academic investigation. The Church's Lord is not a character trapped in a book. The true meaning of the Bible emerges only in the context of prayer and worship, where "dialogue takes place between God and man" (25).

Pastoral Constitution on the Church in the Modern World

The Pastoral Constitution on the Church in the Modern World places the mystery of the Church in the context of a world defined by "the mystery that is man" (*GS* 10). Reminiscent of the council's 1962 "Message to Humanity," the constitution is Vatican II's most daring statement. It is also its longest. It is the longest document produced by any ecumenical council.

The constitution's prologue sets the tone for the document:

The joy and hope, the grief and anguish of the men of our time, especially of those who are poor or afflicted in any way, are the joy and hope, the grief and anguish of the followers of Christ as well. Nothing that is genuinely human fails to find an echo in their hearts (1).

Addressed like John's *Pacem in Terris* to a universal audience, the document offers a unique appraisal of the contemporary human experience and an equally unique response to its problems.

The constitution views the contemporary human situation through the lens of Christian faith. It is not a sociological study of the secular crowd but a theological meditation on the human person. The facts are taken from modern mass society, the meaning from revelation. Jesus Christ is the hinge upon which the constitution turns: "It is only in the mystery of the Word made flesh that the mystery of man truly becomes clear" (22).

Set against the horizon of Christ, the constitution's portrait of humanity is stunning and sobering. The document describes complex creatures made in the image of God, composed of body and soul, endowed with rights, reason, and conscience, and destined for life in community with each other and eternal destiny with God. At the same time, man the sinner suffers from interior conflict and is a "question to himself" (21).

Humans are especially impressive and vulnerable in the modern situation. We are authors and victims of a world "at once powerful and weak, capable of doing what is noble and what is base" (9). Science and technology are signs of our greatness, but they also bring grave risks. The constitution's analysis of atheism is the Church's first systematic study of "one of the most serious problems of our time" (19).

Other issues addressed in the document include marriage, reproductive ethics, economic justice, work and leisure, war and peace, and international cooperation—many of which still dominate Catholic social teaching. The "greatest generation" fathers were particularly precise on total war: "Every act of war directed to the indiscriminate destruction of whole cities...is a crime against God and man" (80). Their honesty about sin in the Church speaks directly to us today:

The Church is not blind to the discrepancy between the message it proclaims and the human weakness of those to whom the Gospel has been entrusted. Whatever is history's judgment on these shortcomings, we cannot ignore them and we must combat them earnestly, lest they hinder the spread of the Gospel (43).

Decrees on Ministry

The nine decrees of Vatican II cover a variety of topics. Five of them deal with pastoral renewal in particular forms of ministry. These documents represent specific applications of the Constitution on the Church.

The Decree on the Bishops' Pastoral Office in the Church, conscious of a "new order of things" in society (*CD* 3), supports new organizational initiatives such as the establishment of national conferences of bishops and the modernization of the Curia. The document places its emphasis, however, on the biblical vision of bishops as apostolic teachers: "witnesses of Christ to all men" (11).

The two decrees on priesthood, Priestly Formation and the Ministry and Life of Priests, also examine practical matters, such as education and formation—and for the same reason: the "vastly changed circumstances" of modern times (*PO* 1). They are at their best when they encourage priests to strive toward "that greater holiness that will make them daily more effective instruments for the service of all God's people" (*PO* 12).

The Decree on the Appropriate Renewal of the Religious Life is the document most concerned with institutional reform. It even gets into the details of the religious habit—long a symbol of Vatican II's impact. Still, its true focus is a balance between *ressourcement*—rediscovering the original spirit of each religious community—and *aggiornamento*. "Before all else, religious life is ordered to the following of Christ…even the best-contrived adaptations to the needs of our time will be of no avail unless they are animated by a spiritual renewal" (*PC* 2).

The Decree on the Apostolate of the Laity challenges conventional notions of the laity's responsibility. Laypeople possess the "right and duty to be apostles" (*AA* 3). Their mission is the mission of the Church: to take Christ into the world. Male and female, young and old, all are invited to think creatively about their potential as "traveling messengers of Christ" in the world (14).

Decrees on Diversity, Unity, and Proclamation

The remaining four decrees highlight the growing edges of Vatican II's theology of the Church. They develop the council themes of unity and outreach, dialogue and mission.

Taken together, the documents on Eastern-rite Catholicism and ecumenism strike the distinctively Catholic note of diversity-in-unity. The Decree on Eastern Catholic Churches honors the Christians of the East in communion with Rome. It expresses great admiration for their different liturgical rites, unique organizations, rich cultures, and distinctive callings—including married clergy (see *PO* 16). Filled with praise for "venerable antiquity" and "ancestral traditions" (*OE* 1, 5), it is the only document untouched by the council theme of updating.

The Decree on Ecumenism advances the quest for Christian unity by identifying "elements and endowments" of authentic Christianity outside the boundaries of the Catholic Church—elements such as confession of Christ, Scripture, baptism, and genuine Christian piety (*UR* 3). The document calls for honest dialogue with Orthodox and Protestant Christians but warns against "false irenicism," friendliness that dismisses fundamental differences (11). Above all, it highlights the spiritual dimension of the task: "There can be no ecumenism worthy of the name without interior conversion" (7).

The last two decrees contribute to the Church's fulfillment of the Great Commission: "Go therefore and make disciples of all nations" (Matthew 28:19). The Decree on the Instruments of Social Communication encourages Catholics to master the art and science of film, radio, television, and other forms of mass communication "to propagate and defend the truth and to secure the permeation of society by Christian values" (*IM* 17).

The Decree on the Church's Missionary Activity matches the council's growing global consciousness with a full-scale theology of global evangelization (spreading the good news). Its main message is the centrality and urgency of the missionary enterprise: "The Church on earth is by its very nature missionary" (*AG* 2). Missionary work should harmonize with the values of ecumenism and recognize "elements of truth and grace" in all religions (9). Salvation is possible outside the Church. The divinely ordained plan of redemption, however, cannot be ignored: "Hence those cannot be saved, who, knowing that the Catholic Church was founded through Jesus Christ, by God, as something necessary, still refuse to enter it, or to remain in it" (7).

The Declarations

The council's three declarations expand the broad-ranging vision of the decrees, reinforcing themes treated in both the Constitution on the Church and the Constitution on the Church in the Modern World. The products of much debate, they contain some of the council's most memorable and provocative statements. They issue from the council's desire to mine reason and revelation and discover "new things that are always in harmony with the old" (*DH* 1; see Matthew 13:52).

The Declaration on Christian Education affirms two fundamental rights: the human right to education (*GE* 1) and the Christian right to Christian education (2). The document is especially important for its defense of the family's divinely determined role in culture. Its definition of true education as the "formation of the human person in view of his final end and the good of that society to which he belongs" (1) runs counter to modern trends that reduce education to the acquisition of specialized knowledge or career skills.

The Declaration on Religious Freedom presents a thoroughly Catholic argument for the rights of conscience. God's revelation to mankind takes form in "one true religion" (*DH* 1), and every person is morally obligated to seek the truth and follow his or her conscience. The dignity and essential freedom of the human person, however, teach us that civil governments do not possess the authority to interfere with the "free exercise of religion" (3)—either of individuals or of groups, including the family. Throughout history, the "leaven of the Gospel" (12) has contributed to the development of these insights in the mind of the Church and of human societies.

The Declaration on the Relationship of the Church to Non-Christian Religions is the council's landmark pronouncement on respect for the world's religious traditions. Pope John Paul II called it "the Magna Carta of interreligious dialogue for our times" (*Ecclesia in Asia*, 31). The document's condemnation of anti-Semitism revolutionized Jewish-Christian relations. Its inclusive view, affirming both the uniqueness of Christ and the knowledge of God outside Christianity, has become one of the most distinctive elements of contemporary Catholic thought:

> *The Catholic Church rejects nothing of what is true and holy in these religions. She has a high regard for the manner of life and conduct, the precepts and doctrines which, although differing in many ways from her own teaching, nevertheless often reflect a ray of that truth which enlightens all men. Yet she proclaims and is in duty bound to proclaim without fail, Christ who is the way, the truth and the life (John 14:6). In him, in whom God reconciled all things to himself (2 Corinthians 5:18–19), men find the fullness of their religious life (*NA 2).*

CHAPTER SEVEN
The Impact of Vatican II

The Second Vatican Council was an event with a beginning and an end. It was also a vision—a luminous articulation of Catholic wisdom, tailored for a particular historical moment and embodied in sixteen authoritative documents. But Vatican II means something else, too. The event and the documents produced a legacy. The legacy of Vatican II has had an impact on Catholic life and thought that stretches far beyond the events of the historic sessions in Saint Peter's and the specific intentions of the bishops and *periti* who authored the remarkable texts.

In his apostolic constitution approving the *Catechism of the Catholic Church*, Pope John Paul II celebrated the "graces and spiritual fruits" emanating from the Second Vatican Council (*Fidei Depositum*, 1). Today, those graces and fruits are all around us. We can also identify challenges and problems that have contributed to the post-council experience. The influence of Vatican II—in its variety and complexity—is powerfully evident in virtually every aspect of our contemporary Catholic experience.

Liturgy

We see the effects of Vatican II very clearly in the worship life of the Church. As we have mentioned, revision of the liturgy was not originally one of the objectives of the council. The Constitution on the Sacred Liturgy approved "restoration, progress, and adaptation" of worship (*SC* 24) but did not issue a blueprint for liturgical reform. Rediscovering the simplicity of ancient worship and adapting the rite to modern conditions only gradually became concerns of the council fathers.

Too often the story of postconciliar liturgical change is filtered through popular myth. History shows no general outcry against Latin, nor did massive change happen overnight. During and after the council, Church leaders experimented with modified liturgies, especially rites in vernacular languages. The turning point was Pope Paul's apostolic constitution *Missale Romanum* (1969). This document, along with a 1970 decree from the Sacred Congregation for Divine Worship, established a completely revised Roman rite designed to preserve the "old" and make use of the "new" (*Cenam Paschalem*, 15). Today the rite is known as the Mass of Paul VI, the *Novus Ordo* (new order) Mass, or simply the "ordinary form" of the Mass.

The revisions began to go into effect on the first Sunday of Advent 1969. The most noticeable features of the rite are now very familiar to Catholics worldwide: the use of local languages, the priest facing the people across a free-standing altar, a generous lectionary of Scripture readings, a biblically focused homily, Communion in the hand and in "both kinds" (bread and wine), an emphasis on liturgy as a community celebration, and the active participation of laypeople.

Paul's revised rite opened a whole new horizon for the Catholic liturgical imagination. Contemporary music, simplified vestments and worship environments, and an air of informality have come to be standard features of the Catholic liturgical experience. Respect for local cultures is also a hallmark of post-Vatican II worship. Laypeople have especially flourished in their new vocations as cantors, lectors, eucharistic ministers, diocesan liturgical directors, and members of parish liturgy committees.

To this day, though, liturgy is a source of both unity and division in the Catholic world. The process of implementing the revisions varied from place to place. In many cases, the revisions were accompanied by a spirit of undisciplined experimentation and an unplanned revolution in Catholic tastes. Critics complain of liturgies held hostage to cultural fads. They also link the revised rite to declining rates of Mass attendance. By the 1990s, some leaders were calling for a "reform of the reform." Pope Benedict XVI has made the revival of reverence and artistic standards in worship a keynote of his pontificate. The debate over liturgy, started in the first session of the council, is far from over.

Doctrine and Theology

The impact of Vatican II has been equally profound in the Church's intellectual life. Changes in the Catholic mind have paralleled changes in the worshipping body. The Vatican II era underscores the truth of the ancient principle *Lex orandi, lex credendi*: "The law of prayer is the law of faith" (*CCC* 1124).

The council's *periti* were in the vanguard of these changes. Some were even catapulted into celebrity status. The Jesuit Karl Rahner, considered by many to be the dean of Catholic theology after the council, hailed Vatican II as the dawn of a new age in Christian thought.

Vatican II transposed Catholic theology into a new key—more in tune with the Bible and the early Fathers but also more attentive to modern science, secular experience, and the insights of non-Catholic traditions. The council strongly endorsed the new biblical, patristic, and ecumenical orientations in priestly education (see *UR* 10 and *OT* 16). It also encouraged laypeople to "take a more active part" in the explanation and defense of Christian ideas (*AA* 6). The Constitution on the Church in the Modern World expressed the hope that more of the laity would devote themselves to theological research (*GS* 62). Since the council, women and laymen have greatly transformed the culture of theology in seminaries and universities.

Catholic intellectual life after Vatican II has especially been marked by pluralism and creativity. The council spoke highly of the "wonderful diversity" of the People of God (*LG* 32) and the "lawful freedom of inquiry, of thought, and of expression" (*GS* 62). It commended "unity in what is necessary, freedom in what is doubtful, and charity in everything" (*GS* 92). Inspired by Pope John's opening speech at the council, many theologians have exercised their legitimate freedom to "seek out more efficient ways...of presenting their teaching to modern man" (*GS* 62). Liberation theology, process theology, and feminist theology represent only a few of the many new forms of the craft energizing Catholic reflection on the faith. Catechists and directors of religious education have also explored new ways to pass the faith on to new generations.

No one at Vatican II, however, imagined that opposition to magisterial teaching would become the widespread phenomenon that it is today. In the 1980s, John Paul II commissioned a new universal catechism in response to a growing crisis of authority and declining levels of doctrinal knowledge. He released the *Catechism of the Catholic Church* on October 11, 1992, the thirtieth anniversary of the opening of Vatican II. Its purpose, he said, would be to "make a very important contribution to that work of renewing the whole life of the Church, as desired and begun by the Second Vatican Council" (*Fidei Depositum*, 1).

Moral Life

No other area of contemporary Catholic experience demonstrates the impact of Vatican II with greater clarity than morality. The "restoration of sound morals" was one of the first goals assigned to the council by Pope John. The greatness of human conscience—"man's most secret core, and his sanctuary" (*GS* 16)—runs like a scarlet thread through all the documents. The chapter on "The Call to Holiness" in the Constitution on the Church is a miniature masterpiece of moral theology. "All Christians in any state or walk of life," it says, "are called to the fullness of Christian life and to the perfection of love" (*LG* 40).

Vatican II awakened many Catholics for the first time to the dignity of their status as responsible moral agents and decision makers. Christian morality, they discovered, is more than blind obedience to rule books or authority figures. The council also introduced many believers to the Church's social teaching—even more robust with Pope John's *Mater et Magistra* and *Pacem in Terris*. After Vatican II, no informed Catholic could ever again imagine that a "merely individualistic morality" (*GS* 30) fulfilled the demands of Christian discipleship. John Paul II's record on human rights and the Church's current leadership in peacemaking and humanitarian efforts would be unthinkable without the council's commitment to social justice.

We need to remember, though, that Vatican II occurred just as a cultural revolution was about to sweep the globe. The council fathers were well aware of the "accelerated pace of history" (*GS* 5). What they did not anticipate were the enormous changes in belief and behavior that would come with the sexual revolution and the women's movement of the 1960s and 1970s. In the public mind, Vatican II's message of moral maturity quickly became confused with secular slogans of liberation and self-expression. Catholic ethics since the council has had to grapple with the meaning of "updating" in a world where people think freedom is license "to do anything they like" (*GS* 17).

The appearance of Pope Paul's encyclical *Humanae Vitae* (1968), reasserting the Church's ban on artificial birth control, exposed an inner conflict within the modern Catholic mind that continues to characterize the post-Vatican II period. A practical consequence of the divided mind has been a significant decrease in the number of Catholics going to confession. Some Catholics have effectively insulated their views on sexuality from contact with the Church's moral witness. Others have redefined Catholic identity without reference to authority or tradition. The sex abuse crisis indicates that even some clergy of the Vatican II generation have not been able to resist the secular world's competing values. A rediscovery of Vatican II's own countercultural impulse will help us chart a new way forward.

Church and World

Simply scanning the landscape of contemporary Catholic life is perhaps the best way to see the full extent of the council's legacy. Imagine Catholic families, schools, parishes, hospitals, charities, missions, seminaries, and universities a hundred years ago. Now picture those institutions today. Vatican II has not only changed the way we worship, think, and behave. It has even changed the way we look.

A major component of the Catholic world is the personnel executing the Church's mission. As we have seen, Vatican II blessed the lay apostolate, restored the office of the permanent deacon, updated religious life, and reinforced the role of the bishop and priest. The council also did much to give birth to the modern papacy. The influx of laymen and women into key positions of leadership—in administration, ministry, education, evangelization, healthcare, and more—vividly illustrates the council's impact on Church structures.

Part of the restructuring has been due to the crisis in vocations. Vatican II noted a "regrettable shortage of priests" (*OT* 6). The fathers, however, did not foresee the postconciliar phenomenon: thousands of priests and nuns leaving active ministry and very few young people filling their positions. Still, council documents offer us sound advice when it comes to revitalizing a culture of vocations: "The duty of fostering vocations falls on the whole Christian community, and they should discharge it principally by living full Christians lives" (*OT* 2).

Another remarkable feature of the Catholic world after Vatican II is its contact with the world at large. Dialogue is one of the great success stories of the council. For decades now, Catholics have contributed to the dialogue between the Gospel and modern culture. Catholic institutions of higher education have poured precious resources into this apostolate.

We have also lived through an almost unbelievable transformation in Catholic relations with other Christians and believers from non-Christian traditions. Two unprecedented events from the pontificate of John Paul II demonstrate just how much ground has been covered since the council. At the 1986 World Day of Prayer for Peace in Assisi, rabbi, guru, swami, minister, imam, and shaman came together at the request of the pope for an unforgettable moment of shared contemplation. On the first Sunday of Lent in the Jubilee Year of 2000, the pope invited all Catholics to pray for forgiveness for sins against the Jewish people and members of other religions. Few events could more forcefully communicate the council's call for an ecumenical "change of heart" (*UR* 8).

Criticism of the Council

Like every ecumenical council, Vatican II has not been uniformly or universally well-received. Critics have complained about liturgy made trivial, doctrine gutted of substance, and heritage put at risk. Most have distinguished between the council itself and a host of questionable experiments conducted in its "spirit."

Many critics have been loyal sons and daughters of the Church. "Absent father" Jacques Maritain mourned the loss of Latin, the fading grandeur of the liturgy, and the declining popularity of Aquinas. Fellow converts Dorothy Day and Thomas Merton expressed similar concerns, despite their support for the council's social agenda. Even Pope Paul admitted that the revised liturgy meant sacrificing great treasure.

More radical critics, called traditionalists or Catholic fundamentalists, reject the legitimacy of Vatican II. French Archbishop Marcel Lefebvre founded his priestly fraternity, the Society of Saint Pius X, as a reaction to the *Novus Ordo* Mass and the documents on ecumenism, world religions, and religious freedom. When he defied Vatican authority and independently consecrated four bishops, he pushed his movement into schism and himself into excommunication. The most extreme traditionalists go even further, claiming that the chair of Peter has been vacant since the death of Pius XII. The popes of the council, they assert, are not genuine successors of the Fisherman.

Interpreting Vatican II

Whether the critics like it or not, Vatican II is here to stay. Its place in history is secure, and its effects—including the unforeseen ones—are largely irreversible. Its language, vision, directives, and what we can even call its style are now part of the tradition that "makes progress in the Church, with the help of the Holy Spirit" (*DV* 8).

A proper understanding of the council is a separate question. Often we use "Vatican II" as shorthand. We describe books, events, initiatives, and sometimes people as "consistent with Vatican II" or "contrary to Vatican II." What we mean when we say these things, however, is not always clear.

Pope Benedict XVI distinguished between two very different approaches to the council in a message delivered shortly after his election to the papacy. One approach he called a *hermeneutic* or interpretation of "discontinuity and rupture." This theory sees Vatican II as a judgment against the past. It divides Catholic history into two main epochs and splits the body of Christ into a pre-Vatican II Church and a post-Vatican II Church.

The problem with this theory, the pope said, is that it distorts what John XXIII and the council fathers said about their own intentions. It reduces the council to a political contest between conservative and liberal interests and turns the mission of the council into an ill-defined quest for all things new. Most importantly, it ignores the supernatural dimension of the Church's mystery.

As an alternative to the theory of "discontinuity and rupture," Benedict proposed a "*hermeneutic* of reform, of renewal in the continuity of the one subject-Church which the Lord has given to us." This approach returns the council to its proper spiritual context and reaffirms the theology of history that guided the council itself. It does not deny the need for periodic reform or restoration but interprets Vatican II in light of Vatican I, Trent, and the whole development of Christian faith, all the way back to Nicea and Jerusalem. "The Church," the Holy Father said, "both before and after the council, was and is the same Church, one, holy, catholic and apostolic, journeying on though time" (*Christmas Address*).

Did the Second Vatican Council, then, make a difference? Yes, absolutely. Every council has. Each has contributed its unique set of graces to the pilgrim People of God. The unity of the Church over time does not mean uniformity. Real change happens, and Vatican II was called to read the "signs of the times" and revive the Church's Gospel mission in order to "serve the men of this age" (*GS* 93).

Did the Second Vatican Council alter the essential nature of the Church or offer a "different gospel" (Galatians 1:6)? No. In the long view, and that is the supremely Catholic view, Vatican II represents one attempt among many to witness faithfully to the "eternal gospel" (Revelation 14:6). Its impact is measured one way by us, another way by "all the Angels and Saints." The Constitution on the Church in the Modern World put it best: "Beneath all that changes there is much that is unchanging, much that has its ultimate foundation in Christ, who is the same yesterday, and today, and forever" (*GS* 10).

Conclusion

From the replacement of Judas to the twenty-one full-scale ecumenical assemblies, Church councils have profoundly influenced our lives of faith, worship, and service. Just a glance at the sweep of Catholic history drives that fact home with clarity. Eliminate councils from Catholic experience, and our religion today—its beliefs, rites, organization, even its art—would be drastically different. Catholic Christianity as we know it would not exist.

Councils have made an especially powerful impact on our sense of spiritual identity. The conciliar principle, weaving in and out of the Catholic story for centuries, reminds us that ours is an uncommon fellowship endowed with supernatural gifts and graced with guidance from above. We remember pivotal moments in our past when an untried course of action "seemed good to the Holy Spirit and to us." We anticipate further development in our attempt to understand more fully and live more faithfully the "mystery of our religion" (1 Timothy 3:16). Councils have made us, and are still making us, who we are as Catholics.

Vatican II was no exception. Contemporary Catholic identity—in all its greatness and even its inner conflicts—has its roots in that extraordinary experience. Our thinking, our worshipping, our serving, our organizing, and even our dreaming have all been marked, and in some cases made, by the council. More than anything, the Second Vatican Council opened a new chapter in the long, evolving Catholic story. Much of that chapter, however, was not scripted by the apostolic churchmen who gathered in Saint Peter's from 1962 to 1965.

Every Catholic around the world—from the 1960s to the present—has helped to cowrite it.

Some pages in the chapter seem almost divinely inspired. Others make us cringe. Vatican II has contributed to the adventure of Catholic history its own curious mixture of "joy and hope" and "grief and anguish." One thing is certain: the chapter remains unfinished. It is only a *schema*. Over time, it will drift toward the middle of the book and take its rightful place in the lengthening story. For now, it is *our* chapter.

Shortly after his election, Benedict XVI, the 265th successor of the Apostle Peter, posed a series of questions about Vatican II to his collaborators in the Curia during a Christmas Address:

What has been the result of the council? Was it well-received? What, in the acceptance of the council, was good and what was inadequate or mistaken? What still remains to be done?

So many years after the council, those questions go a long way toward defining what it means to be Catholic in the present moment. Pope John's prayer on the eve of the "wonderful spectacle" that the Holy Spirit and he conceived can be our prayer now:

*May this council produce abundant fruits: may the light and power of the Gospel be more widely diffused in human society; may new vigor be imparted to the Catholic religion and its missionary function; may we all acquire a more profound knowledge of the Church's doctrine and a wholesome increase of Christian morality (*Journal *391).*

We are still on the slopes of the sacred mountain.

Works Cited

Abbott, Walter M., ed. *The Documents of Vatican II.* New York: America Press, 1966.

Benedict XVI. *Christmas Address to the Roman Curia.* December 22, 2005. http://www.vatican.va/holy_father/benedict_xvi/speeches/2005. Cited as *Christmas Address.*

Catechism of the Catholic Church. 2nd ed. Washington, DC: United States Catholic Conference, 1997. Cited as *CCC.*

The Encyclicals and Other Messages of John XXIII. Ed. Staff of *The Pope Speaks Magazine.* Washington, DC: TPS Press, 1964. Cited as *Encyclicals.*

Flannery, Austin, ed. *Vatican Council II: The Conciliar and Post-Conciliar Documents.* Rev. ed. Northport, NY: Costello, 2004.

John XXIII. *Journal of a Soul.* Trans. Dorothy White. New York: Image Books, 1980. Cited as *Journal.*

Kung, Hans, Yves Congar, and Daniel O'Hanlon, eds. *Council Speeches of Vatican II.* Glen Rock, NJ: Paulist Press, 1964. Cited as *Council Speeches.*

Oder, Slawomir, and Saverio Gaeta. *Why He is a Saint: The Life and Faith of Pope John Paul II and the Case for Canonization.* New York: Rizzoli, 2010.

Paul VI. *Address During the Last General Meeting of the Second Vatican Council.* December 7, 1965. http://www.vatican.va/holy_father/paul_vi/speeches/1965. Cited as *Address.*

Paul VI. *Homily.* December 8, 1965. http://www.vatican.va/holy_father/paul_vi/homilies/1965. Cited as *Homily.*

Suggestions for Further Reading

Alberigo, Giuseppe. *A Brief History of Vatican II.* Maryknoll, NY: Orbis Books, 2006.

Alberigo, Giuseppe, and Joseph Komonchak, eds. *History of Vatican II.* 5 vols. Maryknoll, NY: Orbis Books, 1995–2006.

Bellitto, Christopher M. *The General Councils: A History of the Twenty-one Church Councils From Nicaea to Vatican II.* New York: Paulist Press, 2002.

Hahnenberg, Edward P. *A Concise Guide to the Documents of Vatican II.* Cincinnati, OH: St. Anthony Messenger Press, 2007.

McEnroy, Carmel. *Guests in Their Own House: The Women of Vatican II.* New York: Crossroad, 1996.

O'Malley, John W. *What Happened at Vatican II.* Cambridge, MA: Harvard University Press, 2008.

Ratzinger, Joseph. *Theological Highlights of Vatican II.* New York: Paulist Press, 2009.

Schreck, Alan. *Vatican II: The Crisis and the Promise.* Cincinnati, OH: Servant Publications, 2005.

Sullivan, Maureen. *101 Questions and Answers on Vatican II.* New York: Paulist Press, 2002.

Sullivan, Maureen. *The Road to Vatican II: Key Changes in Theology.* New York: Paulist Press, 2007.